THE NEW FACE OF ENVIRONMENTAL MANAGEMENT IN INDIA

For my mother, who has given me life more than once...

The New Face of Environmental Management in India

AParna Sawhney
Indian Institute of Management Bangalore, India

ASHGATE

Published by
Ashgate Publishing Limited
Gower House
Croft Road
Aldershot
Hants GU11 3HR
England

Ashgate Publishing Company
Suite 420
101 Cherry Street
Burlington, VT 05401-4405
USA

Ashgate website: http://www.ashgate.com

British Library Cataloguing in Publication Data
Sawhney, Aparna
  The new face of environmental management in India. -
  (Ashgate studies in environmental and natural resource
  economics)
  1. Environmental management - India 2. Environmental policy -
  India
  I. Title
  333.7'0954

Library of Congress Cataloging-in-Publication Data
Sawhney, Aparna, 1965-
  The new face of environmental management in India / Aparna Sawhney.
      p. cm. -- (Ashgate studies in environmental and natural resource economics)
  Includes bibliographical references and index.
  ISBN 0-7546-1915-X
      1. Environmental management--India. 2. Environmental policy--India. I. Title. II. Series.

  GE320.I4S28 2004
  333.72'0954--dc22

                                                          2003063567
ISBN 0 7546 1915 X

Printed and bound in Great Britain by Antony Rowe Ltd, Chippenham, Wiltshire

Contents

List of Tables and Boxes

Chapter Tables

Boxes

Appendix Tables

Preface

The globalization era has been a period of accentuated and remarkable changes in the domestic environmental management system in India. Although India has a long history of being a party to all major international environmental initiatives and agreements, the magnitude of the impact on the domestic front had never been as significant as that witnessed in the last decade. Many of the current environmental management practices in India are directly related to global political, economic and social factors. This influence has been reflected in the adoption of common environmental policies in certain export sectors including fishery, textiles and leather products, with export-oriented firms responding to importer demands on environmental product standards.

It must be added, however, that while the Indian environmental management system emerging today clearly reflects the global environmental actions, it has also been largely influenced by an intrinsically domestic environmental consciousness. While common strands in resource and pollution management approaches can be found across countries given the internationalization of environmental issues, the practices that are finally emerging are unique to India. The intriguing question then is: how has environmental management as a whole been affected in India during the last decade of accentuated change?

Liberalization began taking its full form in India in the year 1991, and the analysis in this book concentrates on the regulatory, structural and socio-economic changes that have taken place in the post-liberalization period. In discussing the impact of globalization, the analysis focuses on the changes in government policy, economic structure, firm practices and consumption pattern. The analysis is then taken forward in terms of different stakeholders in environmental management (distinguishing between the government, the firm, and civil society) to discuss the important role played by the Indian community in the new environmental regime.

For a large country like India that defies generalization, the analysis of emerging environmental management is fraught with the complexities of diversity. The common theme emphasized here is that global economic forces have impacted environmental management both in pollution control as well as in the preservation of the indigenous natural resources endowment of India; and the role of the community has been recognized more formally today. Since environmental values have always been ingrained in the daily lifestyle of indigenous communities of India, there is much to be learned from the traditional values and knowledge for evolving a modern day environmental management system. No matter how rudimentary, community participation in environmental management has taken a foothold in India, and this holds a lot of promise in shaping the environmental management regime of the future.

Aparna Sawhney

Acknowledgements

Fourteen years ago at the Delhi School of Economics, my teacher, the late Professor Sukhamoy Chakravarty, first kindled my interest in the field of environment and sustainable development. He has remained a source of powerful inspiration throughout my current work.

It was Professor Jagdish Bhagwati who encouraged me to work in the field of trade and environment at Columbia University, and I would like to thank him for having ingrained in me a unique perspective of free trade.

The initiation of this book project, I owe to my friend and former colleague Professor Steve Pressman, and I would like to thank him.

I would also like to thank Ms. S. Vilasini and Ms. B. S. Nagveni for their efficient secretarial support.

Finally, I must add that I could not have written this book without the support and constant encouragement of my family, including the youngest among them, my five-year old son. My family provided me with ample space and love, and their patience carried me through the project.

Aparna Sawhney

List of Abbreviations

ACMA	Automotive Component Manufacturers Association of India
CAC	Command and Control
CITES	Convention on International Trade in Endangered Species
CPCB	Central Pollution Control Board
CPRs	Common Property Resources
EC	European Commission
EIA	Environmental Impact Assessment
EKC	Environmental Kuznets Curve
EPA	Environment Protection Act
EU	European Union
FDI	Foreign Direct Investment
GATS	General Agreement on Trade in Services
GATT	General Agreement on Tariffs and Trade
GDP	Gross Domestic Product
HACCP	Hazard Analysis Critical Control Point
IFOAM	International Federation of Organic Agriculture Movements
ISO	International Organization for Standardization
JFM	Joint Forest Management
MEA	Multilateral Environmental Agreements
MFA	Multi-fibre Agreement
MNCs	Multinational Corporations
MOEF	Ministry of Environment and Forests
NASSCOM	National Association of Software and Service Companies
NGO	Non-Governmental Organization
ODS	Ozone Depleting Substance
OECD	Organization for Economic Co-operation and Development
PCP	Pentachlorophenol
PIL	Public Interest Litigation
POPs	Persistent Organic Pollutants
PPM	Process and Production Mehods
RBI	Reserve Bank of India
R&D	Research and Development
SC	Supreme Court (of India)
SME	Small and Medium Enterprises
SPM	Suspended Particulate Matter
SPS	Agreement on Sanitary and Phytosanitary Measures
SSI	Small Scale Industries
TBT	Agreement on Technical Barriers to Trade
TED	Turtle Excluder Devices
WHO	World Health Organization
WTO	World Trade Organization

Chapter 1

Introduction

The process of economic development typically leads to environmental degradation, as increased industrialization and consumption lead to the depletion of resources and generation of wastes. It is well established that environmental degradation in the development process results from ill-defined property rights, inadequate pricing of environmental assets (atmosphere, rivers, oceans, land, forests), and distortionary government policies meant to promote growth (like subsidies in the energy, agriculture and transport sectors).[1] These factors affect the nature of the growth of nations by instituting a bias towards polluting industries (like petrochemicals, chemicals, iron and steel, distilleries) and also encourage excessive consumption of polluting goods and services leading to more generation of wastes per capita (like increased vehicular consumption, plastics).

International trade can further exacerbate environmental degradation in cases where the underlying pricing structure fails to internalize environmental cost. Thus countries which do not factor in environmental costs from polluting industries are expected to emerge with a comparative advantage in environmentally damaging activities and subsequent specialization is expected to lead to further degradation of the environment. Similarly, international commerce can drive natural resource-based activities (say, based on forestry, or fishery) to harvest resources in an unsustainable manner. In other words, liberalization can act as a catalyst for environmental degradation, if the pricing structure is incorrect and conservation policies are absent in the domestic economy. Moreover, the larger process of globalization (which encompasses liberalization) aids in the transition of an economy through fundamental changes in a society's perceptions and preferences. In the face of regulatory, economic and social changes taking place, the ultimate effect on the environmental management system of an economy is neither predetermined nor unique.

In the case of a large economy like India, the emerging environmental management system indeed has a unique character that is replete with diversity to match the diversity of the economy and its people. In particular, environmental management in India has undergone radical changes in the last fifteen years. There is an increasing awareness and infusing of environmental aspects into the mainstream management system, whether industry or natural resources, no matter how rudimentary. This development has been accentuated, and sometimes triggered, by the process of privatization and liberalization.

1.1 Liberalization in India

Liberalization in India was initiated in the mid-1980s, took its full form in 1991-92 and still continues. Prior to this, the country followed a protectionist industrial policy with the hope of building a strong industrial structure. The first few economic plans of India (each covering a period of five years, beginning with the first in 1951-52), were guided by economic planning models that explicitly focused on the growth of heavy capital-intensive industries to ensure the establishment of the basic industrial structure in the country (e.g. the Mahalonobis model). It is important to note here that as opposed to the modernization drive adopted in the five-year plans, especially the second and third five-year plans (1956 through 1965), there had been a Gandhian approach to development focusing on voluntary limitation of wants, the need for self-reproducing village communities, and a better balance between man and nature (Chakravarty 1987: 8). Such an ecological approach to the planning process, however, was seen to lack substantive economic foundations (ibid).

The economic model finally adopted, however, did not include on the agenda the issue of internalizing pollution costs of economic development. Thus India succeeded in achieving phenomenal growth of traditional polluting industries (including chemicals, fertilizers, paper and pulp, distilleries) at the cost of environmental damage. Moreover, the growth of small-scale industries (like leather processing and chemical units), primarily to promote employment, added to the generation of untreated hazardous industrial wastes into the ecosystem.

This, of course, is not unique to India, since the industrialized countries too have journeyed through similar development processes, following which remedial environmental policies were adopted by their governments. For instance, in the US and Western Europe, environmental policies and the accompanying growth of the environment industry peaked in the 1970s and 1980s.[2] In the decade of the 1970s, with the 1972 Stockholm Conference on Human Development, India began to establish a more systematic set of environmental regulations to control industrial pollution.[3] The first major challenge to the conventional measure of welfare and quality of life, namely increase in GDP (Gross Domestic Product) per capita, appeared in the same year in *The Limits to Growth* (Meadows et al 1972) that warned of the enormous ecological damage caused by ignoring the carrying capacity of the ecosystem.

By the time India began to liberalize more extensively and systematically in 1991, the government had committed to promoting sustainable development as opposed to only economic development in the country. This implied that intergenerational equity in improving quality of life was as important as improving the quality of life of just the present Indian generation. India thus needed to enforce economic policies and instruments that would ensure that the needs of the present generation could be met without compromising the ability of the system to meet the needs of the future generations. Considering the ecological damage already caused by the growth process during the past four decades, and a commitment to sustainable development, the Indian government began to enhance the set of domestic environmental protection policies and also formalize an environmental action plan.

Domestic regulations on industrial pollution control have been in force in India since 1974; however, the implementation and enforcement of these laws have been poor and violations have been widespread. After the 1984 Bhopal gas tragedy, the government established a more formal structure of environmental protection and also a ministry in charge of environmental policies. The Ministry of Environment and Forests was established in 1985, and it acts as an apex body supervising the activities of the state pollution control boards. One of the most important pieces of environmental legislation to be enacted was the 1986 Environmental Protection Act, under which several environmental notifications have since been passed to augment the current set of environmental regulations.

Privatization and liberalization in India have been accompanied by several positive accompanying features in the overall environmental management system: first, the significance of state-owned enterprises, several of which were polluting in nature, have reduced. For instance, among the large industrial plants violating domestic environmental standards (in terms of installation of pollution abatement equipment) in the mid-1990s, more than half belonged to the public sector (Sawhney 1997b).[4] Similarly, a cross-country industry study of paper mills in four Asian countries including Bangladesh, India, Indonesia and Thailand found that abatement efforts are negatively associated with public ownership (Hartman et al 1997).[5] Liberalization is expected to increase the overall industrial compliance with environmental norms, as ownership changes continue and the private sector increasingly comes under scrutiny.

Second, the processes of globalization and liberalization have increased international market pressure for Indian producers. Outward-oriented Indian businesses have been induced to move towards cleaner products and processes. For example, traditional export commodities like textile, clothing, fish, cereal, beverages, leather, vegetables and fruits began facing environment-related trade restrictions in the developed countries, especially in the 1990s. The OECD (Organization for Economic Co-operation and Development) countries have aggressively pursued the issue of harmonization of environmental standards in trade, fearing that lower standards in developing countries would give an undue comparative advantage to the latter.[6] Indeed, in 1991 legislation was introduced in the US Senate to allow the imposition of special duties on imports produced under environmental standards that are less strict than those in the US.[7]

In India, the threat of losing export markets in the OECD countries has encouraged the environmental up-gradation and certification of products, processes and production facilities. Indeed, the environmental, health and ecolabelling regulations have affected commodities in the major export groups of India. Since the OECD countries as a group absorb more than half of India's total exports, the imposition of trade restrictions on environmental grounds by these countries has had a major impact on the environmental management systems of the export sector. Indian export houses have made efforts in projecting a green face in the world market through endorsed environmental management systems or environmental product certification. For example, Arvind Mills (second largest denim producer in the world) undertook expensive pollution abatement investment to acquire the European Ecotex label to promote its exports. The Indian mill commissioned a plant in 1998 that could boast of being a zero discharge firm.

Third, liberalization has given a boost to the growth of the "clean" service sector, in particular the software industry where global market demand has driven the growth. The businessmen in this industry, the "soft warriors", have created a pool of knowledge workers at a nominal capital cost and have sold their software development and maintenance services to most of the Fortune 500 companies. The expansion of the service sector in India has had two immediate implications for the environment – first, the growth of the economy is less pollution-intensive in the conventional sense (emissions per unit output or per unit labor), and second, the rapid creation of jobs and income increase can be expected to increase demand for environmental quality in the medium and long run (if environmental quality is considered to be a superior good, where demand increases with increase in income).

Increased globalization and liberalization, however, have also been accompanied by apprehensions of adverse domestic environmental effects. The two major fears being: (i) Pollution havens being created in countries with lower environmental standards, which attract dirty industries and specialize in the production and export of pollution-intensive goods; and (ii) Governments lowering environmental standards to attract foreign capital (race to the bottom).

After more than a decade of liberalization, there are questions on what has been the experience in India? Have we been attracting foreign investment in dirty industry and/or specializing in the production of polluting manufacturing goods, since domestic environmental regulations are relatively lax and enforcement poor? Have more stringent international environmental standards been infused into the domestic regulations or have economic growth objectives overridden environmental concerns in India? Meanwhile, is the Indian society aspiring towards an environmentally unsustainable life-style or is it conscious of the environmental costs of growth?

Since the effects of liberalization and globalization are pervasive, to analyze the environmental management system of the country, one needs to distinguish between the different institutional and economic sectors, as well as other stakeholders in the system including the society, and non-governmental organizations (NGOs).

1.2 The Pervasive Nature of Globalization

Globalization has a more pervasive impact across countries in the world than just through trade relationships. The literature has distinguished four main channels for global integration (Panayotou 2000) including (i) economic integration through trade, investment and capital flows; (ii) political interaction; (iii) information and information technology; and (iv) culture. These channels also become the medium of environmental changes in a globally integrating economy. Increased international trade and capital flow accelerate changes in industrial structures in the economy, which directly impact resource use and pollution levels. Moreover, positive income effects brought about by accelerated growth due to trade eventually increase budgetary resources allocated to environmental protection both in absolute terms and relative to GDP (ibid).

Globalization through its political and commercial pressures induces governments to follow more globally oriented environmental policies among others. It is unlikely that governments compete with each other through lower environmental standards, if only to attract foreign capital.[8] Lastly, the increase in information and communication diffuses global consumer taste patterns across national boundaries, which can have beneficial or adverse effects on resource use and pollution, depending on the consumption pattern. The final impact on consumption is however, largely driven by cultural factors.

1.3 Liberalization and Domestic Environmental Effect

Economic literature has shown that free trade per se is not the cause of environmental degradation, although trade policies can be sensitized to ecological concerns. In other words, the presence of environmental distortions in the domestic economy can be accentuated by free trade, thus a trade regime recognizing environmental aspects of trade can help. The causes of environmental problems can always be traced to the improper pricing of the environmental resources, ill-defined property rights, non-internalization of pollution costs by firms, and government interventionist policies (subsidies encouraging activities with adverse environmental effects).

Free trade itself induces environmental changes in an open economy through the structural effect, the scale effect, the technology effect and the product effect (Grossman and Krueger 1991, Veen-Groot and Nijkamp 1999). The structural effect refers to the changes in the composition and location of production and consumption activities. Of course, the environmental impact of structural effect depends on other domestic policies in place, which determine whether environmental costs are internalized or not. The net effect on the local environment will be positive if expanding export sectors are less polluting on average than contracting import-competing sectors; and negative if the opposite holds.[5] Given the pollution coefficients and composition of production, enhanced economic activity (scale effect) is harmful for the environment. However, income growth increases the demand for a cleaner environment, and results in stricter environmental standards and environmentally friendly techniques of production in the domestic economy (technology effect). Hence the technology effect is taken to be positive on the local environment as pollution per unit of output declines. Finally, increasing environmental awareness among consumers is reflected in the consumption pattern (product effect), and trade can have positive or negative effects in affecting preferences. Positive product effect is facilitated by the diffusion of environmentally beneficial goods and services through trade, but negative environmental product effects result through trade in toxic chemicals, hazardous wastes, disease-bearing pests, and endangered species (Adams 1997).

The North-South trade models with environmental pollution typically base the expansion of polluting industries in the developing countries relative to that in industrialized countries. Hence, the local environmental problems are accentuated in developing countries with trade, as they specialize in polluting industries. In such a set up, trade liberalization is detrimental for developing countries (but not for developed countries) when the negative environmental impact from composition and scale effect of trade-induced growth more than offset the positive impact of the technology effect on environment (Copeland and Taylor 1994).

However, the "pollution-haven" hypothesis that developing countries will import pollution-intensive industries through foreign direct investment from industrialized countries, due to the former's lax environmental regulations, has not found much empirical support in the last decade (Dean 1992, Zarsky 1999,

Wheeler 2001). Greater openness, defined by trade regime and foreign investment, for Latin American countries has been associated with a cleaner industry (Birdsall and Wheeler 1992) and pollution havens are more likely to be found in closed economies (ibid, Rock 1996). A cross-country study of pollution intensity of manufacturing output found no evidence that industry has been uprooted from the developed to the developing nations (Lucas et al 1992): even though the pollution intensity of GDP increased in the developing countries during the 1970s and 1980s, it reflected industry expansion as opposed to displacement (migration of dirty industries from the developed countries).

Yet another study, using the World Bank dataset on cross-country pollution intensity of output (but different indicator for trade orientation) found that the pollution intensity of output was indeed higher in open economies as opposed to closed economies (Rock 1996). Whereas, the World Bank research result had indicated that the *rate of growth* of pollution intensity of GDP was lower in open as opposed to closed economies. Another empirical study on trade in pollution intensive goods (environmentally sensitive goods) between 25 OECD and 9 East Asian countries covering the period 1965 to 1995, found no evidence of developing countries having gained a comparative advantage in these goods despite the introduction of stringent environmental standards in the developed countries during the 1970s and 1980s (Xu 1999).

There is a contention that the "pollution haven" hypothesis may not have found support, since studies ignored several important nuances like bureaucratic corruption in host countries that prevent inward FDI (foreign direct investment), and the use of industry-level data masked the phenomenon (Smarzynska and Wei 2001). Using firm-level data, and accounting for corruption levels, and existing environmental standards in 24 transition East European countries, did find a relatively weak support for the "pollution haven" hypothesis, but the results were not robust (ibid).

Local environmental problems like inadequate sanitation and clean water, indoor air pollution from biomass burning, and land degradation, have been associated with a lack of economic development. Research revealed an inverse relationship between these forms of pollution and income per capita (World Bank 1992), implying that economic development goes hand in hand with these forms of environmental quality. For outdoor pollution problems such as atmospheric sulfur dioxide, particulate matter, and metal contamination of river basins, an inverted U-shaped relationship, namely the Environmental Kuznets Curve (EKC), was seen to exist with per capita income (Grossman and Krueger 1994). While environmental degradation increased with the rise in per capita income, beyond a critical level of income, the increase in demand for environmental quality and regulation offset the degradation experienced in the initial stages of growth. This implied that citizens of richer nations are willing to pay more for improving local public goods, like air and water quality, and by analogy as citizens of developing countries become richer they too would increasingly demand a better environment. Underlying the phenomenon of the EKC is another fact, namely that with economic growth, the production structure shifts focus from heavy industries towards the service sector (termed composition change). Moreover change in trade pattern can reinforce the EKC phenomenon as the service-oriented developed economies import pollution intensive output from other (developing) nations (Suri and Chapman 1998, Heil and Selden 2001, Cole and Neumayer 2002).

The EKC studies, however, ignored the underlying structural differences in the countries at different stages of growth and the simultaneous effect of environmental degradation on economic development (Stern et al 1996). Moreover the optimistic result that environmental degradation will reduce with increase in per capita income seems to hold good with OECD data, and that too typically for atmospheric pollution parameters (Stern and Common 2001). Several econometric analyses have concluded, however, that the major results of EKC still hold good, and the composition changes in developed countries seem to arise as a result of an increasing share of imports in the consumption of pollution intensive products.[10]

The question then arises: can developing countries experience the EKC phenomenon and reduce emissions through economic growth to the same extent as the OECD countries? The scope of such replication does not seem optimistic (Cole and Neumayer 2002). However, considering the fact that advanced clean technology is available from the developed countries, developing countries can ride on the cleaner production wave and not follow the same dirty growth path of the industrialized nations (positive externality effect). In other words, technological advancement can lower the social environmental cost of growth such that the EKC shifts downward over time (Panayotou 1992). While clean technology may help, the scale effect of growth in the developing countries is likely to result in severe air and water pollution problems. In this regard, environmental policy (both anticipatory and remedial) can make a difference by reducing the ecological damage during the process of economic growth itself.

The EKC studies are at best representations of experience of different countries over time, and the critical per capita income level corresponding to the peak of the inverted U cannot be considered as some magic number for a turnaround of environmental quality for a particular developing country. The EKC is viewed as showing that environmental degradation is a "growing up" problem to be overcome through rapid economic growth. Thus to the extent free trade speeds up economic growth and raises per capita incomes, any restrictions on trade or diversions of resources away from export-led growth would slow down the transition to a positive income-environment relationship (Panayotou 2000: 5).

Apart from industrial pollution problems, developing countries are typically characterized by open access of common property resources and overexploitation. Thus trade liberalization in these countries also raises the issue of unsustainable resource extraction. The environmental degradation of natural resources in developing countries can be traced to a combination of factors including ill-defined property rights, an erosion of traditional resource management norms, and a large population in proportion to the resource base. Free trade may or may not reduce domestic welfare, depending on the extraction pattern in autarky. Chichilnisky (1994) argued that the tragedy of the commons is exacerbated by trade between the developed and developing nations when the latter specialize in resource-intensive goods because the true price ratios are not reflected in the market. Brander and Taylor (1997), however, showed that, if the countries with open access problems have overexploited their natural resources to a large extent in the absence of trade, then liberalization may ease the environmental problem with the import of the resource intensive goods.

While the above results can be reconciled, it is evident that there is no unanimous answer or outcome as to whether liberalization will lead to a cleaner or dirtier environment in developing countries as they grow. However, it is undisputed that as long as environmental resources are priced correctly (which is quite consistent with differential environmental standards across countries), economic development is good for the environment (working through alleviation of poverty, lowering of population growth rate, and increase in demand for environmental amenities). In such a case, globalization would help the economy to achieve the environmental goal faster. In the global market today, environmental leaders are not less profitable since a good environmental profile is more of an asset to a firm than a liability, notwithstanding the somewhat higher production costs. Green labels sell at a premium in the market and firms with ISO 14000 have some competitive advantages like lower liability insurance, less regulatory oversight, and increased access to customers who care about environmental reputation (WTO 1999).

Global integration helps economies since they tend to set more stringent environmental policies (Wheeler 2001, Fredriksson and Mani 2001). Trade integration tends to reduce lobbying success of the polluting industry lobby, and also creates political pressures to increase environmental standards. Thus, the regulatory gap or the difference between the stringency of environmental standards between industrialized and industrializing countries is likely to be reduced with globalization. Moreover, liberalization can help in achieving a cleaner environment in developing countries in three other ways (Rock 1996): first, the environmental groups in developed nations monitor operations of MNCs in developing countries and threaten green consumerism boycotts in case of bad environmental behavior; second, cleaner technologies will probably have a positive effect; and third, since access to developed country markets depend on compliance with ISO 14000, the new standards may have a significant influence on the local environmental consequences of production in developing countries.

This book analyzes the extent of these developments by tracing the environmental behavior of the industry in India in the post-liberalization period (chapters 4 and 6). It also brings in the increasing community participation in environmental management that has substituted for the lax formal monitoring of polluting firms, whether domestic or Indian subsidiaries of MNCs (chapter 7).

1.4 Global Integration of the Indian Economy

In India, liberalization was initiated in the mid-1980s but has been more systematically pursued since 1991-92. Prior to this, during the industrial incubation period (under protection), if it may be called so, the economy witnessed phenomenal growth in traditional polluting industries like chemicals, fertilizers, paper and pulp, and distilleries, among others. While regulations on industrial pollution control have been in force since the 1970s, the implementation and enforcement of these laws have been poor leading to environmental degradation. The air pollution from industry and vehicles in particular reached appalling levels in certain cities and towns of the country by the early 1990s. For instance, suspended particulate matter, one of the most prevalent air pollution problems in India, in cities like Delhi and Kolkata, measured 460 mg/m^3 (the maximum permissible limit of the WHO being 200 micro grams/m^3).[11] On the other hand, water pollution due to industrial effluents poses grave threats to human settlement since both surface and groundwater have been contaminated.[12] The need for enhancing the country's environmental regulations and increasing the industry's environmental responsibility was recognized, as a result of which the last decade witnessed major legislative changes.

The integration of the Indian economy with the global economy has steadily increased, as is evident from the increase in the relative share of both merchandise trade and FDI to GDP. The share of merchandise trade in GDP increased from 13% in 1990 to 20% in 2000. The change in this index is more significant if the period of comparison is extended to two decades: during 1980 to 1999, the share of trade in GDP increased by about 62%! The share of gross FDI in GDP increased from zero in 1990 to 0.6% in 2000. While foreign direct investment remains small in India compared to some other developing countries like China, the significance of FDI needs to be judged with respect to the situation in the pre-liberalization era. The data is summarized in Table 1.1 below.

Table 1.1 Global Integration of the Indian Economy

Index\Year	1990	2000
Goods trade as % of GDP	13.1	20.3
Gross private capital inflow as % of GDP	0.8	3.0
Gross FDI as % of GDP	0.0	0.6

Source: World Development Indicators, various years.

The magnitude and nature of foreign capital inflow in the post-liberalization era has also changed. The net annual capital inflow was close to US$4 billion during 1991-93, peaked to $12 billion in 1996-97 and has now stabilized at $9-10 billion in the last few years. In the net capital inflow, there has been an increase in the share of non-debt-creating capital like foreign direct investment (FDI), but portfolio investment being volatile by nature has shown sharp fluctuations during the same period. The net foreign capital inflow and the shares of its various components in the post-liberalization period 1991 through 2002 are listed in Table 1.2.

A noteworthy feature of the composition of foreign capital inflow is that external/foreign aid has consistently reduced. The share of foreign aid (external assistance) in net capital inflow dropped from 78% in 1991-92 to 21% in 1995-96. Thereafter foreign aid reduced to less than 10% during 1996 through 2001. In the year 2001-02, the aid component touched 12%.

On the other hand, the share of FDI in total foreign capital inflow registered a dramatic increase from a mere 3% of net foreign capital inflow in 1991-92 to almost 41% in 2001-02. The increase in foreign direct investment has taken the form of green-field investments as well as mergers and acquisitions. Foreign capital has flowed into a variety of industries in India, including telecommunications, transport, consumer goods, chemicals, etc. The industry composition of FDI will be taken up again in chapter 4.

1.5 Growth of the Indian Economy

The growth of the relatively less pollution-intensive service sector in any economy has typically been associated with both a mature stage of development and a move towards a cleaner economic output. Considering the increase in the significance of the service sector in India, one may ask whether a similar deduction can be made here. Has India bypassed the stage of an industrial nation with sound infrastructure,[13] and ventured into the stage of rapidly expanding services sector, with the global corporate ready to tap the large pool of skilled labor?

The growth of the service sector has been continuing since the 1980s, and its share in the total domestic output more than doubled by 1990. A recent empirical analysis of economic growth in India (Nagaraj 2000) shows that, during the period 1980-81 to 1999-2000, the trend growth of the tertiary sector surpassed that of GDP and other sectors. The trend growth rate was 7.1% in the tertiary sector, compared to 5.7%, 3.2% and 6.8% for GDP, primary sector and secondary sector, respectively. After 1991-92, there was a slight slowdown in the growth rate of the secondary sector, and the tertiary sector became the fastest growing sector in the last decade. Indeed the tertiary sector today accounts for about half of the Indian GDP, and there is a growing consensus that the Indian economy is now being driven by services. In 2000, the services sector's value added to GDP was 48%, while those of agriculture and industry were 24% and 27% respectively (see Table 1.3).

Table 1.2   Net Foreign Capital Inflow and Composition, 1991-2002
(US $million and % share)

Capital \Year	91-92	92-93	93-94	94-95	95-96	96-97	97-98	98-99	99-00	00-01	01-02
Net Inflow[a]	3,910	3,876	8,895	8,502	4,089	12,006	9,844	8,565	10,242	9,023	9,545
Of which, %											
1 Non-debt:	3.4	14.3	47.6	57.9	117.5	51.3	54.8	28.2	50.7	56.6	62.1
FDI	3.3	8.1	6.6	15.8	52.4	23.7	36.2	29.0	21.2	26.0	40.9
Portfolio	0.1	6.2	41.0	42.1	65.1	27.6	18.6	- 0.8	29.5	30.6	21.2
2 Debt creating	77.5	39.9	21.3	25.0	57.7	61.7	52.4	62.7	29.5	69.3	14.8
External aid	77.7	48.0	21.4	17.9	21.6	9.2	9.2	9.6	8.8	4.7	12.6
Comm borrowing[b]	37.2	- 9.2	6.8	12.1	31.2	23.7	40.6	50.9	3.1	44.5	-12.0
Short-term credit	- 13.1	- 27.8	- 8.6	4.6	1.2	7.0	- 1.0	- 8.7	3.7	1.2	-9.3
NRI deposit	7.4	51.6	13.5	2.0	27.0	27.9	11.4	20.3	20.9	25.7	28.9
Debt service	- 31.7	- 22.7	- 11.8	- 11.6	- 23.3	- 6.1	- 7.8	- 9.4	- 6.9	-6.8	-5.4
3 Other[c]	19.1	45.8	31.1	17.1	- 75.2	- 13.0	- 7.2	9.1	19.8	-25.9	23.1
Total (1 to 3)	100	100	100	100	100	100	100	100	100	100	100

[a] Net capital inflow is in US$ million.
[b] Commercial borrowing includes medium- and long-term borrowing.
[c] Other capital includes delayed export receipts, advance payments against imports, loans to non-residents by residents and banking capital.

Source: Reserve Bank of India.

The growth of the "relatively clean" service sector is pushing the pollution intensity GDP down. The promise of this effect is significant since India is perceived as a knowledge-based economy in the post-globalization era. This promise is best reflected in the words of former CEO of General Electric, John F. Welch, when inaugurating the company's largest research center outside of the US, in September 2000 in Bangalore, that the real treasure of India is its incredibly skilled workforce. This raw talent is considered to be unique in the world. His classification of India sums up beautifully the image of the latent talent: "*a developing country with a developed mind*"!

Table 1.3 Structure of Indian GDP (% value added to GDP), 1980-2001

Sector\Year	1980	1990	1996	2001
Agriculture	38	31	28	24.5
Industry	26	28	29	27.1
Services	18	41	43	48.4

Source: World Development Indicators, various years.

Yet, the traditional agrarian sector is still important in the Indian economy. Thus the growth of the service sector needs to be viewed along with sectors which continue to be significant. The emergence of the knowledge-based service sector in the economy is juxtaposed with an even larger pool of unskilled labor, and as of today the agricultural sector is still the largest employing sector.

A recent study on the employment effect of liberalization in India indicates that the skilled labor force has benefited more by it than unskilled labor, and the wage differentials between the two groups widened marginally between 1980-81 and 1992-93 (Nambiar et al 1999): the economic growth has been accompanied by polarization even though the proportion of the population living in poverty steadily reduced from 55% in 1973-74 to 36% in 1993-94. The economic growth rate has undoubtedly improved since 1980-81, but there is no sustained reduction in unemployment rates – employment growth has kept pace with the growth in the workforce.

These features are rather disturbing since economic growth was expected to reduce poverty as well as polarization, and according to the growth-environment literature the rise in per capita income would have eventually improved environmental quality (according to the inverted-U EKC). Thus any rapid growth following globalization will have no such neat outcome in India, and the results will at best be mixed. The rural poor will continue to eke out a living from the natural resource base in an unsustainable manner as long as economic growth fails to reduce polarization.

1.6 The Environmental Concerns in India

Environmental degradation in India pertaining to air, water, and land, has resulted primarily from the processes of industrialization, urbanization, growth in population, and erosion of traditional customs and norms (which had earlier helped communities in natural resource conservation). Air pollution problems have been particularly severe in the larger cities (transport and industry sectors being the main sources), while in smaller towns water pollution problems have been more acute (domestic and industrial sectors being the major effluent sources).

Indeed, water pollution is perhaps India's worst environmental problem. The largest contributor to this pollution is the domestic sector, in terms of the volume of wastewater generated in urban India. In fact, the Ministry of Environment and Forests has noted that municipal wastewater accounts for about three-quarters of the total wastewater generation by volume, and almost half the total pollution load. In particular in the Class I cities (population greater than 1 *lakh* i.e. 100,000) in India, about 97.65% of the total wastewater generated by volume comes from the domestic sector, and the rest from the industrial sector.[14]

The treatment status of wastewater generation in all cities across India has been grossly inadequate. In Class I cities, the total available treatment capacity is only 24% of the total volume of wastewater generated. The situation in Class II cities (population greater than 50,000 but less than 100,000) is still worse, with barely 4% of the total wastewater generated being treated, and the rest being disposed of untreated. Untreated wastewater from households and industries has polluted fresh water bodies (lakes and rivers) as well as coastal waters.

Untreated effluents from industry have also caused land pollution and contamination of the groundwater (e.g. nitrate compounds as well as heavy metals). Some of the most polluting industries (air and/or water) identified by the regulatory authorities include: thermal power plants, fertilizer, iron and steel, petrochemicals, chemicals, paper and pulp, and sugar.

Land, surface water and ground water degradation has also resulted from leaching of chemical run-off from agricultural fields. Land degradation is a serious concern in India, since it has led to loss of nutrients and lower food grain production. Besides natural erosion, water logging and untreated effluents, poor land use practices and the excessive extraction of groundwater and deforestation have also led to land degradation.

Deforestation and loss of biological diversity have led to several preservation and conservation initiatives during the last fifteen years, including community participation in watershed programs and regeneration of degraded forests (e.g. Joint Forest Management), specific species projects (e.g. Project Tiger), and ex situ conservation of plant species through institutions across the country.

1.7 The Approach of the Book

As established in the literature, the environmental effects of a globally integrating economy can be traced through different political, structural and cultural channels. Chapter 2 differentiates between the regulatory, structural, and consumption effects of globalization in India, and the following three chapters analyze each of these three effects in detail for India. Chapter 3 documents how the Indian government has been harmonizing domestic environmental legislation under two distinct influences: first under the cooperative commitment made by India under the multilateral environmental agreements, and second, under international trade pressures especially from the OECD countries, where Indian exports have been facing increasing environmental barriers. Chapter 4 focuses on the structural change affecting the environment following the increase in FDI in India and the pattern of Indian exports and specialization. Chapter 5 analyzes how the increase in urbanization and changing consumption patterns in the post-liberalization era in India have aggravated certain pollution problems like that of urban air pollution.

The cumulative effect of environmental initiatives taken by the government, industry and non-government sectors, and the increase in consumer spending on defensive activities (to avoid health damages from environmental degradation) have led to the growth of a new environment industry. Indian businesses have moved towards increased installation of pollution equipment, and environmental certification. The last decade has seen the emergence of a market for pollution abatement equipment, as well as environmental consultation and services in India. Chapter 6 analyzes the growth of the new industry, which is likely to expand with liberalization of trade in environmental equipment and services under the forthcoming WTO negotiations.

In the following two chapters the focus is turned from behavior in the three formal sectors (government, industry and consumption), to the role of the Indian society in environmental management. Chapters 7 and 8 look closely at the Indian community's role in pollution control management and natural resource management respectively. Although the environmental management regime in India qualifies as a command and control regime, chapter 7 analyzes how the community has played an important role in encouraging the enactment of new environmental legislation, and monitoring non-compliant polluting units during the 1990s through the provision of PIL (public interest litigation). Chapter 8 discusses how, in the rural sector, the government has endorsed community participation in an erstwhile-centralized system of natural resource management, notably for watershed and forests. While property rights of these common resources remain with the government, user rights are being shared with village communities in order to develop a participatory management system that would factor in community needs and knowledge in the conservation process.

Globalization has been associated with a boom in information technology and greater access to existing knowledge in the world. Chapter 9 focuses on the state of environmental information in India and also the role played by the NGOs in environmental information dissemination. NGOs have emerged as a significant player in the country's environmental management system, be it in influencing environmental policy making, monitoring polluting industries, encouraging small enterprises to adopt cleaner production, helping villagers to document innovations and practices, or in green rating of market products. In these different capacities the NGOs are playing an important role in disseminating environmental information in India. In a diverse and largely agrarian economy like India, where formal transactions are still significantly absent in the villages, the influence of the external market demand for environmentally sound goods and services is not enough to promote sustainable environmental management. The local market needs to be the driving force, otherwise any positive change achieved with greater openness of the economy will remain as isolated cases. Imparting of environmental education and initiating community involvement in conserving and managing the environment has been facilitated today in the country through the efforts of the NGOs, and promise to have a lasting effect in the development process.

Notes

---

[1] Among the seminal work in environmental economics are: Hotelling (1931) that laid down the economic foundations of exhaustibility of natural resources; Pigou (1932) that established pollution as an externality problem, and distinguished between the private and social costs of an economic activity; Scitovsky (1954) that distinguished between four types of uncompensated non-market externalities between producers and consumers; and Coase (1960) that illustrated how lack of well-defined property rights led to the imposition of environmental damages on society through production and consumption activities (reinforcing and refining Pigou's work).

[2] The concern for environmental pollution, however, is older than the Industrial Revolution! For instance, in 1273 A.D. the air pollution problem from the burning of soft coal led to a series of royal decrees barring the combustion of coal in the city of London. Modern pressures for air pollution control began with the onset of the Industrial Revolution. In 1819, the British Parliament began undertaking studies of pollution abatement measures. (Regens and Rycroft 1988: 5)

[3] Not surprisingly, the Indian environmental regulations lag behind comparable regulations in OECD countries by about a decade.

[4] About 48% of the total non-complying units were under the State (public or cooperative) sector units, 9% were Central public sector units, and the remaining 43% were in the private sector (Sawhney 1997b: 16).

[5] This study included paper mills in the four Asian developing countries; it found that abatement is positively associated with scale and profitability negatively associated with public ownership, and unaffected by foreign links (in ownership, financing or export-orientation). The authors noted that "under some circumstances, communities successfully pressure plants to abate even if little or no support is available from formal regulation".

[6] Harmonization of standards across countries, however, has no theoretical basis. Indeed the diversity of environmental regulations internationally reflects underlying diversity of endowment, technological know-how, and preferences over time and currently between income and pollution of different varieties (Low and Safadi 1992, Bhagwati 1993). "Among dissimilar countries, however, harmonization becomes more intrusive and inefficient" (Low and Safadi 1992: 40).

[7] GATT Report (1992) *Trade and Environment*: page 17.

[8] Bhagwati and Srinivasan (1997) theoretically demonstrated that in a competitive economy with no constraints on the use of tax instruments, capital mobility does not lead to such a "race to the bottom" by governments.

[9] In terms of economic welfare, Pethig (1976) had posed a "fundamental challenge" to liberal trade by showing that in a traditional 2x2 neoclassical trade model with pollution "a welfare loss from trade occurs to one of the countries (necessary condition), if it specializes in the environment-intensive good and if the welfare loss due to the decreased environmental quality overcompensates the welfare gain from the increased quantities of private consumption goods after trade (sufficient condition)". A good was defined to be environment intensive in the model if the labor-emission ratio was less than that of the other good. The fundamental problem, however, was really the non-internalization of the environmental costs in the domestic economy, not free trade per se.

[10] Cole and Neumayer (2002).

[11] *India Today*, December 15, 1996: 47

[12] In the state of Rajasthan, chemical factories in Bichhri completely poisoned the aquifer with untreated effluent discharges. (*Down to Earth*, April 30, 1996: 27, 38).

[13] There is apprehension now that liberalization has shrunk India's manufacturing base in terms of value addition and employment (Nambiar et al 1999). The authors however admit that India's protectionist policy, while encouraging development of an industrial base, resulted in high cost and poor quality industrialization in the sheltered domestic market.

[14] Information based on CPCB (1999a) and (1999d).

Chapter 2

The Three Channels of Change

The processes of globalization and liberalization in India have opened up several channels of change through commerce, governments, and social interactions, which have impacted the country's overall environmental management system. The distinction between the three paths of influence follows closely the effects that stem from the political, economic and cultural linkages of a globally integrating economy. These three channels of change have affected the environmental management system through changes in the domestic regulation (*regulatory effect*) changes in industrial composition and firm practice (*structural effect*), and changes in the domestic consumer behavior (*consumption effect*).

2.1 The Regulatory Effect of Globalization

An open economy, when integrating with the global market, faces political pressures directly as well as indirectly, to move towards harmonization of environmental standards. The widely held perception that developing countries have relatively less stringent environmental regulations is true on the whole, if one were to compare the specific industry/ambient environmental media standards in India versus those in an OECD country. Of course, based on differences in regional environmental resources and the local ecosystem (say the buffering capacity of the different local ecosystems), a completely harmonized set of environmental standards across all countries is neither efficient nor desirable! (Except in the case of public health, where harmonization of standards is desirable.)

The political pressure to upgrade environmental standards in India has taken place largely through: first, the commitments under the multilateral environmental agreements, and second, the commercial interests given the new environmental provisions in the multilateral trade regime of the World Trade Organization (WTO).

The development of a core set of environmental regulations in India began with the preparation for the 1972 Stockholm Conference on Human Development. Although India had enforced several multilateral environmental agreements since the early twentieth century,[1] the Stockholm Conference helped in prioritizing environmental protection and conservation of natural resources within the country. In the two decades following the Stockholm Conference, India developed a complete organizational structure and major domestic environmental legislation. With the next international initiative in the 1992 United Nations Conference on Environment and Development in Rio, India infused the concept of sustainable development with specific country programmes. In 1992 India released the *National Conservation Strategy and Policy Statement*, and the *Policy Statement on the Abatement of Pollution.* Thirty years after the Stockholm Conference, India reaffirmed her commitment to sustainable development in the World Summit on Sustainable Development in Johannesburg in 2002.

The decade of the 1990s, in particular, witnessed a spurt of new environmental laws and amendments of older laws, some of which directly correspond to India's multilateral environmental commitments. Moreover, the government issued guidelines for production process certifications to ensure that environmentally sound production and management practices are adopted in India. This has been particularly significant for the export sector, since the new WTO environmental provisions covered environmental aspects of processes and production methods of traded goods (for example, under the Agreement on Technical Barriers to Trade). The Indian domestic environmental regulations and notifications in the pre- and post-liberalization periods are listed in Table 2.1.

India is a signatory to all major international agreements related to environmental conservation. There are more than 300 multilateral environmental agreements in the world[2] and India is party to about 77 such MEAs (amendments being considered as a separate agreement, since amendments may or may not be ratified by all parties of the original agreement). Some of the most significant MEAs enforced by India are listed in Table 2A.1. More recent MEAs that are set to come into force soon include the Cartagena Protocol on Biosafety (adopted January 2000) and the Stockholm Convention on Persistent Organic Pollutants or POPs (adopted May 2001). For India, commitments to these agreements, especially that relating to POPs, is expected to have significant long-term environmental implications. Table 2A.2 gives the set of pollutants under the POPs convention, and the status of these pollutants in India is taken up in the next chapter.

The Indian experience certainly seems opposed to the hypothesis of "race to the bottom" and instead provides support to the hypothesis that environmental standards become more stringent with globalization. Indeed, political pressures to upgrade environmental standards have accompanied the process of globalization in India much the same way as in other developing countries. In particular, a study on China, Brazil and Mexico noted that at the national level, governments have displayed a consistent tendency to tighten regulation as incomes grow – hence rather than a race to the bottom, it is almost as if "the bottom" has been rising with economic growth (Wheeler 2001). This is also evident in India, as the environmental regulations have been strengthened during the 1990s.

Table 2.1 Indian Environmental Legislation, Rules, and Notifications

Year	Environmental Act/Notification/Rule
1927 :	The Indian Forest Act
1960 :	The Prevention of Cruelty to Animals Act
1972 :	Wildlife Protection Act (amended 1993)
1973 :	The Wildlife (Stock Declaration) Central Rules
1974 :	Water (Prevention and Control of Pollution) Act (amended 1988)
1975 :	The Water (Prevention and Control of Pollution) Rules
1977 :	The Water (Prevention and Control of Pollution) Cess Act (amended 1992)
1978 :	The Water (Prevention and Control of Pollution) Cess Rules
1980 :	The Forest Conservation Act (amended 1988)
1981 :	The Air (Prevention and Control of Pollution)Act (amended 1987)
1982 :	The Air (Prevention and Control of Pollution) Rules
1986 :	The Environment (Protection) Act (amended 1991)
1986 :	The Environment (Protection) Rules (amended 1999, 2002)
1988 :	National Forest Policy
1989 :	The Rules for Manufacture, Use, Import and Storage of Hazardous Micro-organisms, Genetically Engineered Organisms or Cells Rules
1989 :	The Hazardous Wastes (Management and Handling) Rules, (amended 2000)
1989 :	Manufacture, Storage, and Import of Hazardous Chemical Rules, (amended 2000)

Post-Liberalization:

1991 :	The Public Liability Insurance Act (amended 1992)
1991 :	The Public Liability Insurance Rules (amended 1993)
1991 :	The Scheme on Labeling Environment Friendly Products
1991 :	The Coastal Regulation Zone Notification (amended 2001)
1992 :	The Environmental Audit Notification
1992 :	The Criteria for Labeling Cosmetics as Environment Friendly Products
1993 :	The Environmental Standards Notification
1994 :	Environmental Clearance: Restrictions & Prohibitions on the Expansion & Modernization of Any Activity or New Projects (amended 2002)
1994 :	National Ambient Air Quality Standards
1995 :	The National Environment Tribunal Act
1995 :	The Wildlife Protection Rules
1995 :	The Wildlife (Specified Plant Stock Declaration) Central Rules
1995 :	The Wildlife (Specified Plants, Conditions for Possession by Licensee) Rules
1997 :	Prohibition on the Handling of Azodyes

1997 :   The National Environment Appellate Authority Act
1998 :   Bio-Medical Waste (Management and Handling) Rules
1998 :   Order Constituting the Taj Trapezium Zone Pollution (Prevention and
         Control) Authority
1998 :   Ambient Air Quality Standards for Ammonia
1998 :   The Breeding of and Experiments on Animals (Control and
         Supervision) Rules (amended 2001)
1999 :   Environment (Siting for Industrial Projects) Rules
1999 :   Dumping and Disposal of Fly Ash Discharged from Coal- or Lignite-
         based Thermal Power Plants on Land
1999 :   Recycled Plastic Manufacture and Usage Rules
1999 :   Emission Standards for New Generation Sects
2000 :   Municipal Solid Waste (Management & Handling) Rules
2000 :   Noise Pollution (Regulation and Control) Rules (amended 2002)
2000 :   Notification on Laboratories' Use of Pathogenic Micro-organisms or
         Genetically Engineered Organisms or Cells for the Purpose of
         Research
2000 :   Ozone Depleting Substances (Regulation) Rules
2001 :   Batteries (Management and Handling) Rules
2001 :   The Prevention of Cruelty to Animals (Slaughter House) Rules
2001 :   The Eco-sensitive Zone: Mahabaleshwar Panchgani Region
2002:   New Biodiversity Act
2003:   Forest Conservation Rules

Source: Ministry of Environment and Forests.

2.2 The Structural Effect of Globalization

In the Indian development process the basic constraint has been perceived to be that of deficient capital and productive technologies. Moreover, given the high rate of population growth and low land-man ratio, land-saving and capital saving technological improvements have been given precedence in the development process since the beginning of the economic planning process in the 1950s. In the decades of the 1980s/1990s, the liberalization process was conceived to help overcome these constraints, besides encouraging healthy market competition: by encouraging the flow of private foreign capital and ensuring greater accessibility to state-of-the-art technology available in the global market.

The pattern of international trade and investment in turn has directly affected the production structure in the country, which is a crucial determinant of pollution intensity of the gross domestic output. While traditional manufactures like handicrafts, textiles and garments continue to be the significant items in the commodity export basket, a major change has been the emergence of newer export sectors in the invisible category.

Invisible receipts accelerated after 1992-93, and have been led by the inflow of private transfer receipts. Table 2A.3 at the end of the chapter gives the different categories of invisible receipts in the country. However, in the second half of the 1990s, the miscellaneous non-factor service category, in particular led by software exports, grew faster, and during 2000-01 outstripped the private transfer receipts. In 2001-02, miscellaneous services stood as the most important category of invisible receipts. This growth has been aided by the revolution in information technology as well as foreign investment. Foreign capital has come into a diverse set of industries, where the large potential domestic Indian market has been the main mover.

There is no clear indication of the emergence of "pollution havens" in India with liberalization. Moreover the relatively "clean" service sector has developed in leaps and bounds, especially the software sector, riding on the abundance of relatively cheap skilled labor in India. The commodity export basket continues to be dominated by traditional products from handicrafts, textiles, garments, agriculture and allied sectors. Thus, the pattern of both FDI and international trade suggests that there has been no adverse bias towards the polluting sectors in the post-liberalization era.

The implementation of stringent environmental standards in the OECD countries, especially in the food and textiles sectors, has prompted Indian exporters to upgrade their environmental management systems and also obtain international certification. Thus, Indian export businesses (typically the large and medium) have been undertaking investments to project their eco-friendly face in the international market.

The continuing trend in liberalization, and ongoing WTO negotiations are set to encourage international trade especially in environmental goods and services (the latter being one of the service sectors categorized under the General Agreement on Trade in Services, GATS). India, in particular, holds promise with a fast growing domestic environment market in which foreign investors, equipment manufacturers and service providers have already shown a keen interest in establishing businesses.

2.3 The Consumption Effect of Globalization

Finally, besides domestic environmental regulation and production pattern, globalization and free trade policy have affected domestic consumption as well. It is open to question whether the consumption pattern emerging in India in recent years is sustainable. To attain sustainable consumption patterns, it is important to correct the pricing structure, and have a well-informed, environmentally conscious population. Moreover, value systems integrating ecological aspects with lifestyles are important, and need to be promoted (as recognized in Chapter 4 of Agenda 21[3]). Unfortunately, there is a risk that unsustainable consumption patterns experienced in industrialized countries will be replicated in a developing country like India, in the society's pursuit to improve the standard of living guided by those seen in the industrialized societies. On the other hand, there is also the scope of environmental consumer consciousness or green consumerism of the industrialized countries permeating with globalization.

When negative environmental externalities exist in the consumption of goods, liberalization, by making them more readily available (cheaper imports), tends to adversely affect the domestic environmental quality. Unless an optimal domestic environmental policy corrects this, liberalization can lead to lower welfare. This is particularly true for vehicular consumption in Indian cities, where social costs of private vehicle ownership have increased. This phenomenon, however, is not unique to the liberalization era and has been a continuing trend.

More importantly, consumption patterns of a developed country (say, the US) continue to be the benchmark of well-being for consumers in developing countries like India, even though such consumption patterns are deemed environmentally unsustainable. The unsustainability of such consumption stems from the increasing ecological costs per capita, raising questions about whether this actually leads to greater consumer satisfaction or happiness. The move towards a global consumption class in India, however, is peculiar to the more affluent section of the population, especially in the cities. The vast majority of the population still concentrates on the basic subsistence consumption; for example, food accounts for more than half the consumption expenditure of the rural population thus the demand for environmental amenities has a rather long way to go.[4]

With the global community re-evaluating the true measure of well-being (as opposed to runaway consumption) and the merits of traditional community practices, there is promise of evolving a new path of modern sustainable consumption that reduces the ecological costs of consumption per capita. India certainly seems to have a comparative advantage in the ecological value system infused into lifestyles through rituals and community practices (happiness in a frugal lifestyle), which can now be formally recognized and attempts be made to conserve and promote such practices.

Table 2A.1   Selected Multilateral Environmental Agreements Enforced in India

Multilateral Environmental Agreement	Effective	Year signed, enforced
1. Convention Relative to the Preservation of Fauna and Flora in their Natural State (1933)	1936	1939
2. International Plant Protection Convention (1951)	1952	1952
3. International Convention for the Prevention of Pollution of the Sea by Oil (1954, as amended in 1962 and 1969)	1974	1974
4. Plant Protection Agreement for the Asia and Pacific Region (1956)	1956	1956
5. International Convention on Civil Liability for Oil Pollution Damage (1969)	1987	1987
6. Convention on Wetlands of International Importance especially as Waterfowl Habitat (1971)	1982	1981
7. Convention on the Prohibition of the Development, Production and Stockpiling of Bacteriological (Biological) and Toxin Weapons and on their Destruction (1972)	1975	1973, 1974
8. Convention on the International Regulations for Preventing Collisions at Sea (1972)	1977	1973, 1977

9. Convention concerning the Protection of the World Cultural and Natural Heritage (1972)	1978	1977
10. Convention on International Trade in Endangered Species of Wild Fauna and Flora (1973)	1976	1974, 1976
11. Convention on the Conservation of Migratory Species of Wild Animals (1979)	1983	1979
12. United Nations Convention on the Law of the Sea (1982)	1995	1982
13. Statutes of the International Centre for Genetic Engineering and Biotechnology (1983)	1994	1983
14. Convention on Assistance in the Case of a Nuclear Accident or Radiological Emergency (1986)	1988	1986, 1988
15. Convention on Early Notification of a Nuclear Accident (1986)	1988	1986, 1988
16. Protocol on Substances that Deplete the Ozone Layer (1987)	1992	1992
17. Convention on the Control of Transboundary Movements of Hazardous Wastes and their Disposal (1989)	1992	1990, 1992
18. Amendment to the Montreal Protocol on Substances that Deplete the Ozone Layer (1990)	1992	1992
19. Protocol to the Antarctic Treaty on Environmental Protection (1991)	1998	1992, 1996
20. United Nations Framework Convention on Climate Change (1992)	1994	1992, 1993
21. Convention on Biological Diversity (1992)	1994	1992, 1994
22. Convention on the Prohibition of the Development, Production, Stockpiling and Use of Chemical Weapons and their Destruction (1993)	1997	1993, 1996
23. International Tropical Timber Agreement (1994)	1997	1996, 1996
24. International Convention to Combat Desertification in those Countries Experiencing Serious Drought and/or Desertification, particularly in Africa (1994)	1996	1994, 1996
25. Agreement relating to the Implementation of Part XI of the United Nations Convention on the Law of the Sea of 10 December 1982 (1994)	1996	1994, 1995

Note: Two different years in the third column indicate the years of signature and enforcement, respectively, in India. In cases where the two years match, only one year is indicated in the last column.

Source: Compiled from database of Ministry of Environment and Forests, Government of India and the following websites on multilateral environmental agreements: http://www.ecolex.org and http://sedac.ciesin.org/entri.

Table 2A.2 Persistent Organic Pollutants in the Stockholm Convention

Chemical	Activity	Specific exemption
1. **Aldrin**	Production	None
CAS No: 309-00-2	Use	Local ectoparasiticide, insecticide
2. **Chlordane**	Production	As allowed for the parties listed in the register
CAS No: 57-74-9	Use	Local ectoparasiticide. Insecticide. Termiticide in buildings, dams, and roads. Additive in plywood adhesives
3. **Dieldrin**	Production	None
CAS No: 60-57-1	Use	In agricultural operations
4. **Endrin**	Production	None
CAS No: 72-20-8	Use	None
5. **Heptachlor**	Production	None
CAS N No: 76-44-8	Use	Termiticide in structures of houses
		Termiticide (subterranean), wood treatment
		In use in underground cable boxes
6. **Hexachlorobenzene**	Production	As allowed for the parties listed in the register
CAS No: 118-74-1	Use	Intermediate solvent in pesticide
(HCB)		Closed system site limited intermediate
7. **Mirex**	Production	As allowed for the parties listed in the register
CAS No: 2385-85-5	Use	Termiticide
8. **Toxaphene**	Production	None
CAS No: 8001-35-2		
9. **Polychlorinated**	Production	None
Biphenyls (PCB)	Use	Articles in use in accordance with the provisions of Part II of Annex
10. **DDT (Annex B)**	Production	Acceptable purpose: Disease vector control use in accordance with Part II of Annex
CAS No: 50-29-3		Specific exemption: Intermediate in production of dicofol
	Use	Acceptable purpose: Disease vector control in accordance with Part II of Annex
		Specific exemption: Production of dicofol, intermediate
11. **Polychlorinated dibenzo –P-dioxins***	Production	
12. **Dibenzofurans*** **(PCDD/PCDF)**		

The first eight chemicals are for *Elimination*, under Annex A. Annex B chemical DDT (pesticide) is for restricted use.

*Annex C lists chemicals unintentionally produced from anthropogenic sources, like during the manufacture of paper and pulp, incineration of wastes, particularly medical waste containing plastics like polyvinyl chloride.

Source: Stockholm Convention on Persistent Organic Pollutants.

Table 2A.3 Invisible Transactions in India (US $ million), 1970-2000

Category	1970-71	1980-81	1990-91	1995-96	2000-01
I. Non–Factor Services, net	*11*	*1,297*	*980*	*-197*	*2,478*
Receipts	292	2,804	4,551	7,346	18,870
Payments	281	1,507	3,571	7,543	16,392
Of which:					
(i) Travel, net	25	1,107	1,064	1,546	294
Receipts	49	1,221	1,456	2,713	3,168
Payments	24	114	392	1,167	2,874
(ii) Transportation, net	40	7	-110	-158	-1,257
Receipts	145	457	983	2,011	1,913
Payments	105	450	1,093	2,169	3,170
(iii) Insurance, net	0	21	23	36	135
Receipts	16	64	111	179	257
Payments	16	43	88	143	122
(iv) G.n.i.e., net	9	51	-158	-205	316
Receipts	40	111	15	13	657
Payments	31	60	173	218	341
(v) Miscellaneous, net	-63	111	162	-1,416	2,990
Receipts	42	951	1,987	2,430	12,875
Payments	105	840	1,825	3,846	9,885
II. Investment Income, net	*-338*	*325*	*-3,753*	*-3,205*	*-3,821*
Receipts	66	917	368	1,429	2,366
Payments	404	592	4,121	4,634	6,187
III. Private Transfers, net	*116*	*2,693*	*2,068*	*8,506*	*12,798*
Receipts	134	2,707	2,083	8,539	12,873
Payments	18	15	15	33	75
IV. Official Transfers, net	*162*	*750*	*461*	*345*	*336*
Receipts	171	755	462	351	338
Payments	9	5	1	6	2
NET INVISIBLES (I to IV)	-49	5,065	-242	5,449	11,791
Receipts	663	7,183	7,464	17,665	34,447
Payments	712	2,118	7,706	12,216	22,656

Note: Totals may not tally due to rounding off.

Source: RBI *Handbook of Statistics on Indian Economy 2001*, Table 130.

Notes

1 Some of the early multilateral environmental agreements include the *Protocol for the Prohibition of the Use in War of Asphyxiating, Poisonous or Other Gases, and of Bacteriological Methods of Warfare* (1925), and the London *Convention relative to the Preservation of Fauna and Flora in their Natural State* (1933), which were enforced in India in 1930 and 1939 respectively.

2 The complete list of multilateral environmental agreements, and states which are party to the agreements are available in the following websites: http://www.ecolex.org, which lists 480 such MEAs; and http://sedac.ciesin.org/entri, which lists 327 MEAs.

3 Agenda 21 is a comprehensive action plan on development and environment that was adopted by more than 178 Governments (including India) at the 1992 United Nations Conference on Environment and Development in Rio de Janeiro. The global partnership for sustainable development was adopted to prepare the world for the challenges on the 21st Century.

4 The basic amenities to lead a healthy life are largely lacking: during 1990-97 only 19% of the population had access to safe water while 71% had no sanitation (Human Development Report, 1999, UNDP). In comparison, however, the urban population is better off, with 73% having access to improved sanitation facilities by the year 2000 (WRI 2002).

Chapter 3

The Regulatory Effect

3.1 Institutional Structure for Environmental Management

Environmental legislation has a long history in India, and dates back to the nineteenth century. The early environmental legislation, however, was sporadic until the 1970s,[1] after which a systematic set of pollution control laws and environmental acts began to be developed. The Pollution Control Boards at the center and in some states were established with the Water (Prevention and Control of Pollution) Act in 1974. This was followed by The Water Cess Act in 1977, and the Air (Prevention and Control of Pollution) Act in 1981.

In 1980 a Department of Environment was established. In 1984, following the tragedy of the Bhopal gas leak (from the Union Carbide plant) the government decided to establish a full-fledged ministry thus in 1985 a separate apex Ministry of Environment and Forests (MOEF) was formed. The MOEF is an overseeing body that monitors and enforces environmental quality standards in the country through the pollution control boards, and conducts environmental assessments and surveys. The following year, in 1986, an umbrella environmental law, the Environment Protection Act (EPA) was enacted, under which several laws and notifications have been passed since.

The pollution control regime in India is essentially of the command-and-control nature, consisting largely of environmental standards for different industrial activities. The environmental laws are supplemented by fiscal incentives for purchase of end-of-pipe pollution control devices and setting up effluent treatment plants by firms. A more holistic approach has been adopted since 1994, when the submission of an Environmental Impact Assessment (EIA) statement and Environmental Management Plan was made mandatory for any business expansion or modernization, or new project. Depending on the industry sector and size, either the central or the state level authority process the EIA.

Environmental regulation notwithstanding, the pollution problems with respect to air, water, and land have become severe across India. It is evident that the command-and-control nature of the environmental regulations and the lack of enforcement have resulted in environmental degradation. The existing environmental regulations have failed to induce polluters to undertake measures to cut back on pollution or find ways to improve resource efficiency. For instance, air pollution problems are particularly acute in the cities. A study of air quality data for suspended particulate matter in 70 cities of India for 1997 revealed that only 19 cities had pollutant levels below the permissible limit![2] Numerous illegal industrial units in urban India discharge untreated effluents into the atmosphere, rivers and land. In some cases legislation is also incomplete: for example, while the Water

Act covers industrial effluent standards, it ignores the domestic and municipal effluents even though they constitute 90% of India's wastewater volume!

The regulatory changes taking place in the country can be considered to be those stemming from intrinsically external factors like globalization and trade liberalization and those that have followed from internal forces like community pressures. This chapter analyzes the Indian regulatory impact of globalization, and later chapters (7 and 8) take up the public participation in environmental management, which reflect the intrinsically domestic forces that have affected the environmental institutional system in the country.[3]

In other countries, it has been documented that when effective national environmental regulation is absent or weak, local community pressures often succeed in changing the industry's environmental performance. For example, studies in South and South-East Asian developing countries suggest that despite the lack of effective regulation, environmental performance of many firms has improved (Hartman etal 1997, Hettige et al 1996). In India, community pressure has been associated more with environmental public interest litigation (taken up in detail later in chapter 7), non-governmental agencies (NGOs) and judicial activism, which have substituted for the laxity of formal monitoring and enforcement of environmental standards in the economy.

Formally, the Ministry of Environment and Forests has acknowledged the vital role of NGOs in environmental management of the country, and the Central Pollution Control Board has an NGO cell through which NGO help is solicited for environmental awareness campaigns in the country. While the economic policy changes with globalization have direct impact on environmental management practices in the organized sectors, changes in environmental management of the rural sector are being brought about more effectively with a participatory approach wherein grassroots level activity of NGOs complement the current environmental regulatory regime.

3.2 Effect of Globalization on Domestic Environmental Regulation

Domestic environmental regulation in India has been affected by global integration and trade liberalization. This section concentrates on incidences of environmental stringency following greater global integration as well as trade liberalization.

The literature on the impact on environmental legislation from globalization recognizes that the major forces work through the following (Panayotou 2000):

(i) economic growth leading to more stringent standards and enforcement;
(ii) environmental measures included in regional and bilateral trade agreements.

Moreover, there is increasing evidence now that environmental policy formation is affected by the degree of openness, particularly in developing countries. Fredriksson and Mani (2001) observed that trade integration is a significant factor responsible for increasing environmental stringency (an index measure) in a sample of 50 developing countries.[4]

In India, the increase in domestic environmental legislation in the 1990s followed from the commitments made in the international environmental initiatives, first those falling directly under multilateral environmental agreements (MEAs) and second, initiatives to protect export interests due to new environmental provisions under the multilateral trading system of the World Trade Organization (WTO). The analysis here distinguishes between these two routes of change since both are integral to the globalization process.

The commitments under the MEAs are reflected in the nature of environmental characteristics covered in the new domestic legislation. For instance, the environmental acts and notifications in the 1970s and 1980s covered intrinsically domestic pollution problems, especially those of air and water. In contrast, the domestic initiatives and legislation of the 1990s cover aspects of sustainable development and global environmental concerns as well as the depletion of the ozone layer, loss of biodiversity, patenting of biological resources etc, which fall under the more recent MEAs ratified by India.

The second distinct influence on domestic environmental legislation is directly linked to the international trade sector. Some of the environmental notifications in the 1990s have resulted from environment-related trade restrictions on Indian exports in the OECD countries. The health and environment related trade restrictions on Indian exports have increased the pressure for upgradation of processes and production methods both in the food and non-food sectors. There has been a move towards food-safety procedures (like Hazard Analysis Critical Control Point), upgrading environmental management systems (like the voluntary ISO 14001), as well as obtaining environmental certification and labels. The government has set up environmental testing and certification laboratories, and has helped in environmental training. Opening of the economy has thus directly put pressure on raising environmental standards in order to maintain access to major export markets.

3.2.1 Commitments under MEAs

In the twentieth century, multilateral environmental agreements emerged as a cooperative approach to joint responsibility of nations towards preserving the global environmental resources. For more than fifty years now, India has participated in several global environmental initiatives in the form of multilateral environmental agreements (MEAs). Beginning with the 1933 Convention on Preservation of Fauna and Flora, India has been a signatory to and has ratified most major multilateral environmental agreements. In the previous chapter, Table 2A.1 listed some of the major MEAs that India has been party to (acceded, signed or ratified). Commitment and ratification of an MEA often entails corresponding domestic legislation. Thus India's increasing commitment to global environmental protection is reflected in the corresponding increase of domestic environmental legislation in the decade of the 1990s. A brief analysis of the domestic legislation corresponding to five of the major MEAs is discussed below:

(i) *The Convention on International Trade in Endangered Species of Wild Fauna and Flora (1973):*

India ratified the Convention on International Trade in Endangered Species of Wild Fauna and Flora (CITES) in 1976, the year it came into force. The CITES sought international cooperation for the protection of certain species of wild fauna and flora against over-exploitation through international trade. This is reflected in the Indian Wildlife Protection Act (1972, amended 1993), which provides a detailed list of different wildlife species that are protected and considered to be the property of the state governments. All dealings in trophy and animal articles are prohibited without license in India.

In particular, Chapters V and VA of the Act lay restrictions and prohibit trade in animals and animal trophies (listed in Schedule I or Part 11 of Schedule II). Effective 1972, under the Act, no person is allowed to:

> acquire, receive, keep in his control, custody or possession, sell, offer for sale, or otherwise transfer or transport any animal specified in Schedule I or Part 11 of Schedule II, any uncured trophy or meat derived from such animal, or the salted or dried skin of such animal or the musk of a deer or the horn of a rhinoceros, except with the previous permission in writing of the Chief Wildlife Warden or the authorized officer (Section 40, *Wildlife Protection Act 1972*).

(ii) *The Basel Convention on the Control of Transboundary Movements of Hazardous Wastes and their Disposal (1989):*

The Basel Convention came into force in 1992, and India ratified the agreement the same year. The corresponding domestic environmental legislation, namely the Hazardous Waste Management Rules Act (1989) encompasses some of the Basel provisions related to the notification of import and export of hazardous waste, illegal traffic, and liability.

The Hazardous Waste Management and Handling Rules 1989 (amended 2000) lists the hazardous wastes that can be imported and exported in conformation with the Basel Convention. The 2000 Amendment specifies that:

> any occupier exporting or importing hazardous waste from or to India shall comply with the articles of the Basel Convention to which the Central Government is a signatory (Rule 11, *Hazardous Waste Management and Handling Rules*).

(iii) *The Montreal Protocol on Substances that Deplete the Ozone Layer (1987)*

India acceded to the Montreal Protocol along with its London Amendment in June 1992, the year the Protocol came into force, and in 1993 the Country Program for phasing out of ozone depleting substances (ODS) was approved under the Protocol. The Ministry of Environment and Forests established an Ozone Cell, and also the Steering Committee on the Montreal Protocol to facilitate the implementation of this program.

The corresponding domestic environmental legislation is the Ozone Depleting Substances (ODS) Rules 2000 (under the 1986 Environment Protection Act). The

ODS Rules 2000 refers to the Montreal Protocol in the main text of the legislation with respect to phasing out ozone depleting substances in production and consumption, lists the substances identified under the Protocol, and also lists the signatories of the Protocol.

(iv)   The Convention on Biological Diversity (1992)

India ratified the Convention on Biological Diversity (CBD) in 1994, the year it came into force. The CBD focuses on three core areas, including conservation of biodiversity, sustainable use of biological resources and equitable sharing of benefits arising from their sustainable use. Thus the Convention covers issues on habitat preservation, intellectual property rights, biosafety, and indigenous peoples' rights.

India's regulatory initiatives in the conservation of biological diversity are evident over the last three decades, following the Stockholm Conference on Environment and Development in 1972. The Stockholm Conference had emphasized environmental protection and conservation of natural resources in national priority. The Wildlife (Protection) Act of 1972 (amended 1991) provided the domestic legislation to protect wild animals, birds and plants, including their habitat. In 1976, the 42nd amendment of the Indian Constitution observed that:

> the State shall endeavor to protect and improve the environment and safeguard forests and wildlife in the country and protect and improve the natural environment including forests, lakes, rivers, wildlife and have compassion for living creatures (*Articles 48a and 51A g*).

The New Biodiversity Act 2002 follows directly from the 1992 United Nations CBD. Indeed, radical changes in the Indian institutional structure of environmental management have resulted from the CBD in conjunction with the WTO Agreement on Trade Related Intellectual Property Rights (1995). The domestic legislative bills triggered by India's commitment to these two agreements affect natural resource management systems since it fundamentally changes the property rights framework. For instance, the Protection of Plant Varieties and Farmers' Rights Bill (2001), and the Biological Diversity Act (2002) introduce sovereign rights and private property rights for biological resources and related knowledge. The first bill provides incentives for the development of the commercial seed industries. The bill recognizes the farmers' rights like that of breeders; however, there are apprehensions that the registration criteria including novelty, distinctiveness, uniformity and stability may pose difficulty for the indigenous Indian farmers to obtain property rights. Despite large-scale public protests and apprehension in India, the endorsement of a new regime reflects regulatory commitment under the MEAs.

There have been other related regulatory initiatives to preserve habitats for conserving biological diversity in India. There are restrictions and/or environmental clearances mandated for development projects located near Reserve Forests and ecologically sensitive areas including National Parks, Sanctuaries and Biosphere Reserves. Moreover there are now certain specific ecologically sensitive areas identified across the country where economic and industrial activities are restricted/prohibited. Some of these notifications include: Dahanu Taluka (in the state of Maharashtra) declared as an Ecologically Fragile Area (1991, amended

1999); restricting location of industries, mining and other activities in Doon Valley (1989); No Development Zone at Numaligarh, East of Kaziranga (1996), and the Pachmarhi Region as an Eco-sensitive Zone (1998).

(v) The Stockholm Convention on Persistent Organic Pollutants (2001)

Table 3.1 Status of Twelve POP Chemicals in India

Chemical	Status	Notification date
Aldrin	Complete ban on manufacture, use, import and export.	September 20, 1996
Chlordane	Complete ban on manufacture, use, import and export.	September 20, 1996
Dieldrin	Use restricted for locust control in desert areas by Plant Protection Advisor to GOI.	May 15, 1990
Endrin	Complete ban on manufacture, use, import and export.	May 15, 1990
Heptachlor	Complete ban on manufacture, use, import and export.	September 20, 1996
Hexachlorobenzene	Complete ban on manufacture, use, import and export. (Has never been manufactured in India.)	n.a.
Mirex	Never registered in India.	n.a.
Toxaphene	Complete ban on manufacture, use, import and export.	July 27, 1989
Polychlorinated Biphenyls	Banned for use and import since 1990. Has never been manufactured by India, but imported, according to Ministry of Chemicals and Petrochemicals. According to the Ministry of Environment and Forests, however, no PCBs have been manufactured or imported since 1965.	1990
DDT	Banned for agricultural use and restricted use in public health sector.	May 26, 1989
Polychlorinated dibenzo –P-dioxins*	Data not available	
Dibenzofurans*	Data not available	

Source: Srishti-Toxics Link (2000): pages 9-10.

Although the Stockholm Convention on Persistent Organic Pollutants (POPs) has not come into force as yet, this multilateral environmental agreement is set to bring in major changes in India (the agreement was signed in 2002). The agreement focuses on reducing and eliminating the release of the 12 toxic POPs (called the Dirty Dozen, listed in Table 2A.2).[5] The POPs treaty is especially important for developing countries like India, since the chemical degradation associated with the use of these toxic chemicals, which the industrialized countries have experienced, can be avoided during the process of industrialization in developing countries.

Table 3.1 lists the eight of the dirty dozen that are already banned in India and the effective date of the ban or restriction (see Table 2A.2 on POPs listed in the Stockholm Convention). Two of the 12 POPs were banned in 1989, but most of these chemicals were banned in the 1990s in preparation of the formal commitment. Since India has signed the Convention, a national action plan to phase out the POPs will be made. As per the commitment, India will restrict, phase out and ban the production and use of POP pesticides and POP industrial chemicals; minimize releases of POPs as unwanted by-products, and where feasible, prevent or avoid their generation. Obsolete stocks of POPs have to be properly destroyed. It appears that commitments under the POPs will help India to leapfrog into an industrializing path which is cleaner (since industrialized countries now need to clean up POPs generated or used indiscriminately in their development process).

3.2.2 Domestic Regulation Following Environmental Trade Restrictions

Apart from multilateral environmental agreements, the environmental provisions in the multilateral trading regime have also provided a channel of influencing domestic environmental regimes. Multilateral trading rules have changed fundamentally since 1995 under the WTO to accommodate differential environmental standards, certifications, and consumer risk preferences across nations.

Under the General Agreement on Tariffs and Trade (GATT), only Article XX allowed for departure from free trade in goods, to protect the environment and human health, provided such measures did not constitute arbitrary or unjustified discrimination between countries where the same conditions prevail, or a disguised restriction on international trade. Compared to the GATT, the new provisions under the WTO have increased the scope of production process-related trade restrictions based on environmental and health grounds. While there are no explicit environmental agreements, a number of WTO agreements that came into effect in 1995 have environmental provisions. These include, among others, the Agreements on the Application of Sanitary and Phytosanitary Measures (SPS), Technical Barriers to Trade (TBT), Agriculture, Subsidies and Countervailing Measures, Import Licensing Procedures, and Safeguards. Of these, the environmental provisions under the two agreements SPS and TBT have been most extensively used. While these two agreements were meant to prevent protectionist practices and make the multilateral trading system more transparent vis à vis the use of health and technical measures, they have now legitimized trade barriers based on non-product related process and production methods as compared to the GATT regime.

In the second half of the 1990s, Indian exports began facing entry barriers in the OECD markets under the provisions of the WTO agreements on TBT and SPS – including stipulations on labeling, chemical pesticide, genetically modified organisms, etc. The threat of losing market access to the OECD countries has induced regulatory changes in India to improve the quality and safety standards of both production processes and products for export. The provision under GATT Article XX has also been invoked to restrict exports from India: the most noteworthy case being that of the Shrimp-Turtle dispute. The export of manufactures like leather and textile products have also been adversely affected by stringent standards effective in these countries, and consequently led the Indian government to ban certain hazardous chemicals in production processes.

The stringent food safety and quality standards have adversely affected agricultural and allied exports from India. In particular, Indian food consignments have been rejected at port in the US, EU and Japan on safety and quality grounds (analyzed in detail in Chapter 4). Since agricultural and allied exports form a significant part of the total export basket (albeit less significant than the manufactured items), this has prompted the government and its affiliated export institutions to take steps to address the problem. There is now an effort to harmonize food safety and quality standards within India, and to club the various domestic regulations (pertaining to food safety and quality) under a common order. The government is considering establishing a Food Regulation Authority (FRA), to formulate and update food standards for domestic and export markets. One of the objectives would be to harmonize the Indian standard with the quality norms of Codex Alimentarius Commission (MFPI Annual Report 2001-02).

3.2.2.1 The Case of the Shrimp-Turtle Dispute

There has been a progressive change in the interpretation of the exceptions to free trade under the GATT Article XX. Today, unilaterally environmental trade barriers under Article XX may be allowed even if it impinges on intrinsically domestic policies of the member country on which it is imposed, in effect falling in the extrajurisdictional domain of the country taking the unilateral measure. This is particularly evident from the nuances of the legal interpretation of the article in the verdicts of Tuna-Dolphin I and II under the GATT as opposed to the more recent WTO dispute verdicts of Shrimp-Turtle I and II. All four cases involved the use of unilateral import restrictions by the US against developing country exports that use environmentally damaging production processes.

In the Tuna-Dolphin case, the US slammed the import restrictions on tuna from several Latin American countries on the grounds that the tuna harvesting methods (by using purse-seine nets) killed more dolphins than acceptable by US standards (under its Marine Mammal Protection Act). In the Tuna-Dolphin I (1991) ruling, the GATT dispute settlement panel found the US embargo unjustified under the principle of national treatment (Article III), which required equal treatment of home and imported products and the production method regulations of the two countries did not matter. The ruling implied that Article XX could not be used by a member country to enforce its own laws regarding animals or exhaustible resources outside its own jurisdiction. In the Tuna-Dolphin II (1994) case, although the US embargo was found to be in violation of GATT provisions, the ruling was more equivocal, stating that unilateral trade measures might be permitted in other cases.

In the Shrimp-Turtle case, the US banned shrimp imports from South Asian countries, including India, since the shrimp trawlers (by not using turtle excluder devices) killed too many Olive Ridley turtles than acceptable by US standards (under its Public Law 101-162, section 609). The US shrimp import ban was invoked in 1996, and India (as well as Malaysia, Pakistan and Thailand) requested a WTO Dispute Panel against the unilateral import ban.

In the Shrimp-Turtle I (1998) case, the dispute settlement panel considered the WTO as an integrated system and used all articles, agreements, preambles and annexes to judge the case. The US import ban was found unjustified, not because the trade sanction was unrelated to the intrinsic characteristics of the traded good, but because the US did not indulge in cooperative efforts to protect Olive Ridley turtles prior to the sanction. In effect the judgement left open an avenue for similar unilateral actions, as Barfield (2001) observed, the Shrimp-Turtle I case set forth an "evolutionary interpretation of unilateralism", and this could trump earlier rules.

Subsequently in the Shrimp-Turtle II case (2001), both the WTO Panel and Appellate Body found the US measures banning shrimp imports from Malaysia as justified under Article XX of the GATT 1994, since the US was found to have engaged in *good faith efforts* to protect the Olive Ridley turtles. The Shrimp-Turtle II ruling thus represented a clear move away from the GATT understanding that trade rules would not regulate process and production methods (PPMs) as understood under the Tuna-Dolphin I case.

During the Shrimp-Turtle I dispute settlement, India argued that TEDs (Turtle Excluder Devices) are not the only means of protecting sea turtles. Moreover the mere use of TEDs in mechanized shrimp trawlers is a rather narrow approach to the bigger issue of protecting the coastal environment (Olive Ridley turtles being part of the coastal ecosystem). In particular, Olive Ridley turtles are listed as an endangered species under Schedule I (*Part II Amphibians and Reptiles*) of the Indian Wildlife Protection Act, 1972.

Before the 1996 WTO Shrimp-Turtle dispute, a distinct legislative movement had started in India for the protection of the coastal environment, including the Olive Ridley turtle: after commercial shrimp farming started taking off in India in the mid-1980s, environmental and social groups took exception to the adverse impact, both on the fragile coastal ecosystem as well as on the traditional fishermen. In 1994, a public interest petition was submitted by one such group,[6] which sought the enforcement of the Indian Coastal Zone Regulation Notification (1991), to stop intensive and semi-intensive type of prawn/shrimp farming in the ecologically fragile coastal areas, and to impose a prohibition on shrimp farming in wastelands or wetlands. The petition also requested the constitution of a National Coastal Management Authority to safeguard the marine life and coastal areas.

The Supreme Court passed several orders (1994 through 1996) against establishment and even demolition of shrimp farming in the delicate regions of the coastal states, and the eco-restoration of the damaged environment by the shrimp farmers.[7] Subsequent to the 1996 Supreme Court judgement, the Aquaculture Authority was set up within the Ministry of Agriculture (under the Environment Protection Act 1986), to execute the court order and promote sustainable shrimp aquaculture in India.

Box 3.1 Protecting More Than Just the Olive Ridley Turtles

The protection of Olive Ridley turtles had been under the purview of Indian legislation long before the 1996 WTO Shrimp-Turtle dispute. These turtles are listed under Schedule I of the Indian Wildlife Protection Act (1972); and Appendix I of CITES (ratified by India). In India, the largest known population of Olive Ridley turtles is found in the eastern state of Orissa. In 1975, the Gahirmatha coast in Orissa was spotted with the world's largest nesting ground for these turtles, and subsequently two more rookeries were found in Orissa. The Orissa Marine Fisheries Regulations Act (1982) and Rules (1983) banned fishing within 5 kms of the coast, and the Coastal Regulation Zone notification in 1991 (under section 3 of the Indian Environment Protection Act 1986) prohibited several activities within the 500-meter area of the coast.

In the early 1990s, a movement to protect coastal environment and traditional fishing communities against commercial marine farming began in India. Social action groups in the states of Orissa, Andhra Pradesh and Tamil Nadu joined in the campaign against shrimp industries. In 1994, a public interest petition was filed in the Supreme Court under Article 32 of the Constitution of India to prevent unsustainable shrimp farming in the coastal ecosystem. The Supreme Court judgement in December 1996 ordered the demolition of all aquaculture farms by March 1997, which were violating the Coastal Regulation Zone notification of 1991. In another case, in 1994, WWF India filed a petition against the state of Orissa for violation of the 1972 Wildlife Protection Act, 1980 Forest Conservation Act, 1991 Coastal Regulation Zone notification, and for threatening the existence of the mangrove ecosystem. In 1998, the Orissa High Court issued directions in favor of the WWF petition, that all fishing trawlers have to be equipped with TEDs. Subsequently, Orissa was the first Indian state to bring in TED technology, and adapt it to the requirements of the Indian fishermen. In 1997, the Orissa government declared the Gahirmatha coastline as a marine sanctuary with no mechanized fishing allowed within 20 kms of the coast. These legislative initiatives were highlighted in the WTO Shrimp-Turtle dispute settlement to show that endangered species can be well protected by other means than Turtle Excluder Devices (TEDs), and that measures were already under way in India.

The movement against mechanized shrimp farming in India has centered on the issues of environmental security, social justice and survival of traditional small fishing communities, besides the protection of turtles. There is no denying, however that the WTO dispute helped publicize and heighten the focus on this broader issue in India, and facilitated legislation in Orissa to protect the coastal ecosystem, including the Olive Ridley turtles.

Source: Ministry of Agriculture (2002); CSE (1998), Behera (2000), Kachhapa (2000).

Meanwhile in 1996, the state of Orissa, which harbors the largest known population of Olive Ridley turtles in India, declared 65,000 hectares in Bhitarkanika and Gahirmatha regions as sea turtle sanctuary (notification number 7FY-SE(H) 49/95-60-FARD dated January 1996). Mechanized fishing was banned within 20 kms of the coastline. The timing of the new regulation coincided with the dispute at the multilateral trade forum, and India quoted the new domestic legislation at the WTO dispute settlement as part of the domestic efforts in protecting the coastal ecosystem and Olive Ridley turtles in particular.

Eventually, the WTO Dispute Panel, as well as the Appellate Body, judged the import prohibition unjustified (in 1997 and 1998), since the US had not indulged in cooperative efforts with the Asian countries to protect turtles prior to the sanction – and not least because of India's domestic efforts! In 1998, however, TEDs were made mandatory for shrimp trawlers in Orissa in response to a domestic petition (see Box 3.1). More recently in 2001, as part of a larger country-wide effort to develop a sustainable model for conservation of endangered marine reptiles and their habitats along the Indian coastline in ten states of India, Olive Ridley turtles in Orissa were tagged for documentation of their migration and nesting habits.

In India while much of the effort in conservation of the Olive Ridley turtles is derived from larger environmental initiatives, the WTO dispute certainly helped to bring the regulator's attention to these issues. The domestic socio-economic and environmental concerns, however, are broader and include the protection of traditional fishing communities and the mangrove ecosystem. In particular, shrimp culture and mechanized fishing for exports have faced increased scrutiny from environmental groups due to their adverse environmental impact on the mangrove and coastal ecosystems. The WTO dispute seems to have increased the publicity of the domestic conflict between commercial/ mechanized fishing and the protection of the coastal ecosystem along with its traditional coastal communities.

3.2.2.2 Other Environmental Initiatives and Trade Restrictions

There are other instances where environmental notifications have been issued in India following environmental trade restrictions on Indian exports in the OECD countries. In 1989, Germany (followed by Denmark, Sweden and the US) banned the toxic fungicide pentachlorophenol (PCP), and leather exports from India, which still used PCP in processing, were adversely affected. Subsequently the use of PCPs in tanning was banned, and the government helped in the import of PCP-substitutes for the industry.

Similarly, the presence of azo dyes in textile and leather articles was the basis of export rejects in Europe in the 1990s. In March 1997, the Ministry of Environment and Forests banned the use of azo dyes in textile articles, leather clothing and shoes (under Section 6(2) (d) of the Environment Protection Act and rule 13 of Environment Protection Rules). The phasing out of azo dyes has had a positive effect of inducing dye manufacturers to look for alternatives within the country like eco-friendly natural dyes. Thus, higher environmental standards abroad prompted new legislations to help the export sector in India, and have led to more stringent domestic standards in the last decade.

3.3 Moving Beyond the End-of-pipe Regulations

Some of the new environmental notifications in the 1990s incorporated environmental management guidelines for economic activities. The nature of the Indian environmental regulations, while being focused mainly on the installation of end-of-pipe pollution control equipment, has of late changed somewhat towards a more holistic environmental management approach, incorporating compulsory environmental impact assessment and audit. Environmental audit (under Environmental Protection Rule 14) became effective in 1993, and in 1994 environmental clearance was made mandatory for industrial activities. In 1994, environmental impact assessment (EIA) was made mandatory for 30 categories of developmental activities to ensure that development options are environmentally sound and sustainable, including industrial projects, thermal power plants, mining projects, river valley hydro-electric schemes and infrastructure projects.[8] Similarly, the Bio-medical Waste Rules (1998), and Hazardous Waste (Management and Handling) Rules (amended 2000) have helped to attract more equipment manufacturers with consulting services in the Indian environment sector.

The liberalization in multilateral trade of goods and services today include the environment sector. Indeed the potential of environmental markets in developing countries like India is largely perceived to have followed from the increasing stringency of environmental regulations. The current WTO negotiations in the environmental sector encompass a broad definition of the sector of both environmental products and services, going beyond the end-of-pipe pollution abatement approach to include pollution prevention and resource efficiency. In particular, the definition of environmental products and services encompasses two significant characteristics, namely: first, efficient resource management, emphasizing resource productivity; and second, clean technology, i.e. pollution prevention as opposed to just pollution abatement and cleaning-up operations. The broader definition today fits well with the concept of sustainable development, which is one of India's primary goals. With further commitment to liberalization, especially in the environment sector, the environmental management regime is set to move beyond the end-of-pipe pollution command-and-control management regime.

Notes

[1] Earlier environmental legislation was scattered and not under a common umbrella (see Shaman 1996 for details).

[2] "Deadly Particles", *Down To Earth*, December 15, 1999.

[3] One can of course argue that some of the actions of the local community can well be influenced by the globalization process itself, and thus the term "intrinsically domestic" may not be true. While acknowledging the possibility of such effects, the analysis here does not deal with the sociological roots of such processes.

[4] Their complete model actually tests for the impact of political stability and corruption levels on environmental policy formation as well. More globally integrated economies tend to set more stringent environmental policies, particularly in politically stable countries. Trade integration tends to reduce lobbying success of the polluting industry lobby.

[5]   Pesticide residue in food in India has adversely affected both the domestic and the external sectors. Contaminated food has affected the health of even babies, since human milk and fat from many parts of India have shown high levels of pesticide content. Research has shown that newborn babies take in 40 times the safe levels of DDT through mother's milk (TERI Newsletter May 2002 quoting the *Toxicology Atlas of India: Pesticides, 1990*). In the export sector, Indian consignments of beverages and food have been rejected due to high levels of pesticide residue.

[6]   The Writ Petition No 561(C) in 1994 was filed by Mr S. Jagannathan, Chairman of *Gram Swaraj Movement*, a voluntary organization for the upliftment of the weaker sections of society.

[7]   The respondent states to the petition included Gujarat, Maharashtra, Orissa, Kerala, Tamil Nadu, West Bengal, Goa, Pondicherry, Daman/Diu, Andaman/Nicobar and Lakshadweep. The final Supreme Court Order in 1996 was based on a variety of reports, including those of the inspecting committee, the National Environmental Engineering Research Institute as well as the UN. The 1995 Report of the Court's inspecting committee (inspection conducted in the states of Andhra Pradesh and Tamil Nadu) recognized the damage to the land and water ecosystems and observed: "The cost for eco-restoration of the coastal fragile area must be borne by individual entrepreneurs of the coastal aquaculture farms in keeping with the Polluter Pays principle." It also prohibited commercial coastal aquaculture even beyond 500 metres high tide line unless a comprehensive and scientific Environmental Impact Assessment (EIA) Study had been conducted by the entrepreneur, and the Environmental Management Plan approved by the respective State Departments of Environment, Pollution Control Board, Shore Development Authority, and also by the Ministry of Environment and Forests. (S. Jagannath versus Union of India, 1994 Writ Petition 561, *Aquaculture case*, http://www.elaw.org/resources).
       Subsequently, in 1997 the Ministry of Agriculture and others filed a review petition of the 1996 Supreme Court judgement, and a stay order on the demolition of shrimp farms (located in the sensitive coastal zone) was obtained. The Aquaculture Authority also submitted an Environment Impact Assessment Report to the Court in 2001 (Ministry of Agriculture 2002).

[8]   MOEF Annual Report 2000-01.

Chapter 4

The Structural Effect

4.1 Structural Effect in Investment and Trade Patterns

One of the main objectives of the new economic policy package in 1991 was to bring in foreign capital, resource-saving technology and an increase in merchandise and service trade. A decade of liberalization has seen significant growth in both trade and investment. However, while the role of foreign direct investment (FDI) as a source of long-term capital has been increasing in the country, the total FDI inflow has hovered around US$2 billion per year since the mid-1990s (except for 1997-98 when it touched $3.5 billion, *Reserve Bank of India*). Moreover, the share of FDI in total investment is still less than 5%.

The systematic liberalization followed through the 1990s has led to considerable expansion in trade and foreign capital flow. In particular, during 1990-2002, the share of exports (and imports) in the gross domestic product increased from 5.8% (and 8.8%) in 1990-91 to 9.3% (and 11.9%) in 2001-02. Foreign investment too registered considerable increase: from a mere 0.03% of GDP in 1990-91, it increased to 1.2% in 2001-02 (see Table 4.1).

Table 4.1 Indicators in the External Sector (in percent), 1990-2002

Indicator	1990-91	1999-2000	2000-01	2001-02
Trade				
Exports/GDP	5.80	8.4	9.8	9.3
Imports/GDP	8.80	12.4	13.0	11.9
Invisibles				
Invisible Receipts/GDP	2.40	6.8	7.6	7.4
Invisible Payments/GDP	2.40	3.9	5.0	4.5
Invisibles (Net)/GDP	-0.10	3.0	2.6	2.9
Capital Account				
Foreign Investment / GDP	0.03	1.2	1.1	1.2
Foreign Investment / Exports	0.60	13.8	11.4	13.2

Source: Data in Table 6.1 of RBI Annual Report 2001-02.

The environmental impact of FDI depends on various factors: the sectors of investment, age of the facilities, parent firm policies and strategies, the degree of export orientation of the investment, host country environmental regulations and degree of enforcement, home country regulations regarding the responsibility of MNCs shareholders for overseas operations, etc (Chudnovsky and Lopez 1999).

In this chapter the environmental aspects of the accompanying economic structural changes following liberalization in India are examined through:

(i)   the composition of FDI in terms of capital being attracted in traditional polluting industries or cleaner industries,
(ii)   the environmental performance of foreign subsidiaries in India,
(iii) the composition of Indian merchandise exports in the post-liberalization period to analyze whether specialization has moved towards polluting goods, and
(iv)   the recent emergence of a "clean" service export sector.

4.2 Foreign Direct Investment

Foreign direct investment provides an additional source of capital formation in an open developing economy that can help promote growth. Foreign firms have the potential to make a positive contribution to environmental improvement by encouraging flow of better technology, management practices, and by providing competition to the erstwhile complacent firms in the host country, thereby inducing these firms to also upgrade. Finally, by generating employment directly and indirectly in related industries, FDI can reduce poverty, and the positive income effect in turn can increase demand for a better environment.

Yet, as the barriers to foreign capital flow began to be progressively reduced in developing countries in the 1990s, apprehensions of potential adverse effects on the environment became a major issue of concern. In particular, the role of FDI as a vehicle of creating pollution havens in developing countries became one of the most contentious issues in the debate on environment versus trade: that "dirty industries" would migrate from developed to developing countries due to lower environmental standards in developing countries.

Several studies, however, indicated that since pollution abatement costs of industries in the OECD countries are only a few percentage points of the total production costs, it is unlikely that relatively lower environmental standards would be the moving force for migrating industries (Jaffe et al 1995). Not surprisingly, abatement costs did not have any significant impact over time on the revealed comparative advantage in the sectoral trade of the US (Ferrantino 1997) since the overall abatement costs were too small to determine comparative advantage. In particular, the US pollution abatement costs rose from 0.3% of output value in the 1970s to 0.8% in 1992 for manufactures (only the capital expenditure for abatement was significant, and equal to 10% of total capital costs). As for FDI, there is still no clear evidence of an increasing flow of pollution-intensive industries into developing countries assumed to have more lenient environmental regulation. Within certain industries, there have been instances of foreign investment encouraging the installation of polluting units in developing countries, but not at the macro-economic level. Thus, Zarsky (1999) observed that even if the regulatory gap between the OECD and the developing countries is large, the total environmental spending by OECD firms apparently is too small to matter and encourage a relocation of polluting firms from developed to developing countries.

4.2.1 FDI in India by Source Country

The research on pollution abatement and pattern of capital outflow in the US (Jaffe et al 1995, Ferrantino 1997) has significance for India, since the US continues to be the single largest source of foreign capital into India. The US accounted for a fifth of total approved FDI in India during the last decade (followed by Mauritius, the UK and Japan): about 20% of approved FDI, and 16% of actual foreign capital inflow during 1991-2001.[1]

Table 4.2 gives the breakdown of country-wise actual FDI inflow during 1994-2001, and also ranks the source countries by their cumulative share in the 7-year period. The six countries listed accounted for three-quarters of the total FDI inflow in the last seven years: Mauritius, the US, Japan, Germany, the Netherlands and South Korea. While it appears that capital inflow from Mauritius is steadily increasing, many investors located in the US and Europe route investments through Mauritius for tax benefits. The US is ranked as the second largest source of foreign capital in India in the table, with a share of 19% of total FDI inflow in the last seven years, but it may well be the largest source given that Mauritius is an intermediate country.

Table 4.2 Foreign Investment Inflows[a] in India by Source Country, 1994-2001
(US $ million, and percentage)

Country	94-95	95-96	96-97	97-98	98-99	99-00	00-01	Cumulative[b]	Country Share[c]
Mauritius	197	507	846	900	590	501	843	4384	34.3
USA	203	194	242	687	453	355	320	2454	19.2
Japan	95	61	97	164	235	142	156	950	7.4
Germany	34	100	166	151	114	31	113	709	5.5
Netherlands	45	50	124	159	53	82	76	589	4.6
S Korea	12	24	6	333	85	8	24	492	3.9
Others	286	482	576	562	470	462	378	3216	25.1
Total	872	1,418	2,057	2,956	2,000	1,581	1,910	12,794	100.0

[a] Excludes inflows under the Non-Resident Indian direct investment route through the Reserve Bank and inflows due to acquisition of shares under Section 29 of FERA. All figures have been rounded off to the nearest whole number. The data for the year 2000-01 is provisional.
[b] Cumulative capital inflow from each country over the 7-year period 1994-2000.
[c] Percentage share of each country in the cumulative capital inflow over the 7-year period.

Source: Computed from data in *RBI Annual Report*, various years.

Even in terms of portfolio investment, US-based foreign institutional investors (FIIs) seem to be the leaders, though these investments are often routed through Mauritius. India's tax treaty with Mauritius in 1982 grants exemptions from capital gains tax and offers concessional rates of dividend tax on investment from that country. Thus, in the post-liberalization period in India, offshore business entities of FIIs began routing investment through Mauritius to take advantage of the tax shelter.[2]

Most of the foreign investment in India is destined for the union territory of Delhi, followed by the states of Maharashtra, Karnataka, Tamil Nadu and Andhra Pradesh. In terms of location of industries within India, there is no evidence of new firm location being affected by differential environmental enforcement across the states. An establishment-level study covering the five most polluting sectors, including chemicals, rubber, paper, metals and non-metallic minerals, found that plant location is significantly positively related to the level of environmental spending by the state government (as a proxy for stringency) after controlling for the several factors across states (Mani, Pargal and Huq 1997). The study indicated that interstate difference in stringency of environmental enforcement within India does not seem to be an important factor for investors in potential site considerations.

4.2.2 Sector Composition of FDI in India

The industries of major interest to foreign investors in India include relatively "clean industries" (in terms of pollutant emissions per output) like telecommunications, computer hardware, software and services, and environmental equipment and services. The New Industrial Policy of India in 1991 opened up a whole range of industrial activities to foreign investment. Foreign capital is now allowed in financial services, retail banking and insurance. The liberalization regime opened up sectors that were earlier monopolized by the state, including power generation, telecommunications, oil and natural gas exploration. Projects for electricity generation, transmission and distribution, roads and highways, ports and harbors, vehicular tunnels and bridges were permitted foreign equity participation up to 100% (provided the foreign equity does not exceed Rs 1500 crores, one crore being 10). More recently, the scope of FDI has been further enhanced in sectors that were earlier "reserved" for small-scale enterprises (e.g. in textile and garments).

Consider the industry composition of approved foreign direct investment in India in the last decade: Table 4.3 lists the industry share of approved FDI over the period 1991-2000. The most significant features of the annual approved FDI by industry are that: the share of the services sector increased from 3.6% in 1991 to 32% in 2000, and the share of the power and fuel sector rose from a mere 0.4% to 16% in 2000. This trend is reflected in the cumulative share of each industry over the 10-year period (last column of Table 4.3), with the service sector, and the power and fuel sector each accounting for 28% of the total approved investment. This is followed by electrical machinery and transportation, accounting for 10.6% and 7.5% respectively.

The traditional polluting industrial sectors of chemicals, rubber, paper, metals and non-metallic minerals certainly do not seem to be of prime interest to the foreign investors in the recent past, since the combined share of these industries has been 15.7% of the total investment over the 10-year period. The individual shares being 6.3% in chemicals, 5.8% in basic metals, 1.8% in non-metallic, 1.3% in paper and 0.5% in plastic and rubber.

It should be noted, however, that the pattern of approved FDI and actual FDI inflow are not quite comparable, since often inflows constitute barely 20% of the approved FDI. Delays depend on the nature of investment projects, as well as on bureaucratic factors. Table 4.4 gives the industry composition of actual FDI in India over seven years since 1994-95, when FDI inflows became more significant. The categories of industrial sectors listed in Tables 4.3 and 4.4 are not identical. For instance, for actual FDI inflows in Table 4.4. Power and fuel is not reported as a separate category by the Reserve Bank of India, but it is listed in Table 4.3 for approved FDI.

In terms of actual FDI inflows during the last seven years, the two industries of Engineering (21.3%) and Services (17.3%) can be ranked as the largest recipients of foreign capital in India, followed by Electronics/electrical equipment (12.5%). Interestingly, the rank of Chemical and allied products remain in fourth place under both approved FDI and actual FDI (received 11% of the total foreign capital inflow).

Considering the fact that the four sectors of Engineering, Services, Electronics/electrical equipment, and Computers together account for 57% of the total FDI inflow during the last seven years, it is clear that India has attracted investment in sectors utilizing skilled labor. The domestic environmental regime (considering it is more lax than in the industrialized countries) certainly does not seem to be a significant factor affecting capital inflow into India.

Table 4.3 Industry Share in Approved FDI (percentage share), 1991-2000

Industry \Year	1991	1992	1993	1994	1995	1996	1997	1998	1999	2000	Cumulative*
Service	4	10	18	12	61	30	18	21	26	32	28.4
Power & fuel	0	39	32	17	16	16	48	45	20	16	28.0
Electrical machinery	20	12	7	4	5	9	5	6	9	34	10.6
Transportation	4	4	3	8	4	8	7	5	22	3	7.5
Chemicals	28	12	5	12	4	9	6	7	3	5	6.3
Basic metals	0	2	14	17	1	6	5	7	5	5	5.8
Food, agricultural	11	11	13	5	3	10	6	2	1	1	4.8
Non-electrical machinery	11	3	2	6	3	2	2	2	2	1	2.1
Other non-metallic	5	1	1	4	1	2	1	1	4	1	1.8
Misc. industries	12	2	2	5	0	2	1	1	3	2	1.6
Textiles	3	4	1	7	1	1	1	1	1	1	1.4
Paper	1	1	1	2	0	3	1	0	2	0	1.3
Plastic-Rubber goods	0	0	1	0	0	1	0	2	0	0	0.5
Total	100	100	100	100	100	100	100	100	100	100	100.0

*   The last column has been computed to give the cumulative share of each industry for the ten-year period 1991-2000.
   Annual figures in the first ten columns pertain to the industry share in that particular year, rounded off to the nearest whole number, thus 0 implies a share of less than 0.5%.

Source: Calculated from data in *Foreign Trade and Balance of Payment*, CMIE, July 1999: 450-5, and July 2001: 350-51.

Table 4.4   Industry Share in Foreign Investment Inflows[a] (percentage of total), 1994-2001

Industry\Year	1994-95	1995-96	1996-97	1997-98	1998-99	1999-00	2000-01	Cumulative[b]
Engineering	15	18	35	20	21	21	14	21.3
Electronic/ electrical equipment	6	9	7	22	11	11	11	12.5
Chemical /allied products	16	9	15	9	19	8	7	11.4
Services	11	7	1	11	18	7	12	9.7
Finance	11	19	11	5	9	1	2	7.6
Computers	1	4	3	5	5	6	16	6.0
Food & dairy products	7	6	12	4	1	8	4	5.5
Pharmaceuticals	1	4	2	1	1	3	3	2.3
Others	31	24	14	24	13	35	30	23.6
Total	100	100	100	100	100	100	100	100.0

[a]   Excludes inflows under the NRI direct investment route through the Reserve Bank and inflows due to acquisition of shares under Section 29 of the Foreign Exchange Regulation Act.

[b]   This column gives the cumulative share of foreign capital inflow in each industry for the seven-year period, while figures in the first seven columns correspond to the industry share in that particular year. Data for 2000-01 is provisional.

Source: Computed from capital inflow data in *RBI Annual Report*, various years.

In particular, the industry-wise investment flow from the US, the single largest source of foreign capital in India, has been in power and oil refinery (39%), followed by food processing industries (11%), telecommunications (10%), services (9%), and electrical equipment including computer software & electronics (8%).[3] Moreover, the ranking of sectors in India for the US investors indicates that the information technology (IT) sector is one of the most attractive markets in India, and others include: pollution control equipment; telecommunications services and equipment; computers and peripherals; education; biotechnology; power transmission and distribution. The market size of the IT sector has grown from US$5.23 billion in 1999-2000 to US$8.26 billion in 2000-2001 reflecting a growth of 58%,[4] and estimated to be US$9.62 billion in 2001-02. More recently, for the year 2003, the US Department of Commerce ranked the Indian environment sector as the second most attractive sector after computer software services[5] for American exporters and investors.

4.2.3 Firm Behavior of MNC Subsidiaries in India

While it is obvious that there has been no polluting sector bias in foreign investment in India, the question still remains as to whether global companies consider a developing country like India as a "pollution haven". In other words, since environmental regimes are lax in a developing country like India, even if investment bias towards dirty industries does not exist at the country level, are polluting practices rampant at the firm level? Do foreign firms indulge in polluting practices by using outdated technology in India?

Country-level studies indicate that foreign investment does not affect pollution abatement expenditure. Hartman et al (1997) examining the paper and pulp plants in four developing Asian countries including India, found that foreign ownership, financing or links to OECD markets did not affect the firm level environmental performance (although the sample size was small and only four out of the 26 plants had foreign ownership). Another study on industrial pollution in Indonesia during 1989-90 (Pargal and Wheeler 1995) noted that newer plants are cleaner (whether domestic or foreign), and the multinational ownership has no independent effect. This would seem logical for India too, since newer firms face stricter environmental norms with increased regulatory measures, judicial activism as well as environmental NGO monitoring. Thus the research at World Bank inferred that while foreign investment can be valuable for many reasons, it is unnecessary for effective pollution control at the firm level (World Bank 2000: 116).

Ideally, subsidiaries of multinational companies (MNCs) in developing countries have the potential to bring in better environmental practices in their host countries. However, as a survey (Zarsky 1999) noted, there is little evidence that foreign firms consistently perform better in developing countries. Independent surveys in India corroborate the fact that environmental management seems to be no better in firms with foreign ownership when compared to that in domestic firms. Yet at the same time, there is no evidence that India is a pollution haven.

There are instances of both state-of-the-art facilities being built in India, as well as instances where MNC subsidiaries have dumped untreated wastes callously outside the factory walls. For instance, in March 2001, the Indian subsidiary of the Anglo-Dutch company, Hindustan Lever Mercury Thermometer Factory at Kodaikanal, was exposed by Greenpeace to have dumped mercury wastes outside the factory premises in torn sacks. The factory suspended operations shortly afterwards in June 2001.

In India, a survey on environmental management of MNC subsidiaries in Delhi and Maharashtra (the two regions where FDI is concentrated) found that subsidiaries largely benchmark their environmental performance to other comparable Indian firms (Ruud 2002). The sample consisted of 53 OECD MNC subsidiaries. The survey revealed that local environmental management systems of MNC affiliates are rarely certified, and the domestic market orientations made these firms operate in a more isolated manner from global competition and the general requirements of the world market. The main motivating factor for improved environmental performance in India was attributed to pressure from the headquarters (50% of surveyed firms), followed by 'current or future regulatory pressure' (23%), local management leadership (12%), and NGO pressure (6%). The factor of "pressure from the headquarters", however, may also contain pressure from international environmental NGOs, since parent companies are only too well aware of the scrutiny by NGOs and the potential threat of discredit in their home countries in case they are found to be polluting in poorer countries.

Ruud (2002) reported instances of companies applying chemical inputs in India, which would not be allowed in equivalent European facilities. However, there was no evidence that such an opportunity to pollute has been a driving factor in locating MNC units to India. This basically reflects the fact that the formal Indian pollution control regime is more lax than those in the parent countries, and the MNCs have exploited this to their benefit in their operations.

Yet, Ruud (2002) contends that the MNCs are not necessarily using India as a dumping ground for obsolete and polluting technologies. The survey shows that although only a few of the studied MNCs imported state-of-the-art environmental control equipment, various state-of-the-art procedures were observed. In other words, the environmental management of these units is being strengthened, and the major driving force seems to be the intra-firm dynamics between corporate headquarters and affiliated Indian units. This is evident in the form of environmental auditing and reporting procedures: about three-quarters of the sampled firms have systems where on-site environmental auditing is conducted by corporate headquarters (ibid: 108). This is a positive change observed in recent years since none of the affiliated Indian units had environmental policies prior to 1991. Thus while the actual environmental performance of MNC subsidiaries in India is disappointing, the survey does suggest that environmental management systems have at least been adopted in the corporate agendas of the 1990s.

4.2.4 Technological Issues

The optimistic view that FDI is a potentially powerful instrument in promoting sustainable development through transfer of environmentally friendly technologies and practices across borders is not evidently significant in developing countries. The empirical evidence on the environmental impact of MNCs on host developing countries is at best mixed: there are instances of MNC subsidiaries using obsolete (and hence "inferior") technology, as well as using greener technology and better environmental management practices in East Asian and Latin American countries (Chudnovsky and Lopez 1999).

In India, FDI continues to cater to the domestic market, thus the pressure of upgrading technology/management practices is not as high as it would have been had production been geared towards the global market.[6] For instance, in the consumer car sector, which experienced a significant market growth with foreign investment, a study in 2001[7] found that the current engine design is at least a decade old compared to similar types of vehicles manufactured in the industrialized countries. This exactly matches the lag in the vehicle environmental standards (for example Euro II) between India and the industrialized countries. Moreover, FDI flows to India remain small compared to other countries, and also in relation to the domestic capital formation.

As for facilitating the adoption of modern technology in the post-liberalization period in India, it seems that purchase of technology (equity-based) has taken precedence over R&D and in-house technology generation. With liberalization, the relative price of foreign technology has declined versus developing one's own technology, and Indian firms have opted more for equity-linked technology transfer, while pure technology licensing collaborations have declined dramatically in the 1990s (Basant 2000). There is also a concern that since foreign investors opt for sole or joint ventures to one time technology transfer, local affiliates of foreign companies may neither have the freedom nor the incentive to invest in R&D in India (Rao et al 1999). However, even though real growth in R&D expenditure in the private sector was lower in the 1990s compared to the 1980s, some industries registered faster growth in the last decade compared to the 1980s (Basant 2000). These included telecommunications, agricultural machinery, dyestuff, drugs and pharmaceuticals, textiles, soaps and cosmetics, glass and cement. Basant (2000) observed that competition in some of the industries increased due to the entry of MNCs, and change in certain industries, like in the dyestuff industry, seems to be in response to the challenge from environmental regulation. Thus, there is some evidence of positive spillovers of foreign R&D expenditure on domestic firms.

4.3 Pattern of Indian Exports

Apart from the apprehension of dirty industries migrating across borders through investment, another environmental concern has been the issue of developing countries specializing in pollution-intensive goods. With lax pollution norms and under-priced natural resources, the trade versus environment debate of the 1990s had suggested that developing countries would find a comparative advantage in producing and exporting polluting goods (like leather and chemicals) or natural resource intensive goods (like timber). This section focuses on the pattern of Indian commodity exports to discern whether exports from traditionally polluting industries have grown, and also discusses the emergence of new export sectors in the post-liberalization era in India.

A study of five particularly pollution-intensive industries including iron and steel, non-ferrous metals, industrial chemicals, pulp and paper, and non-metallic products, shows that a shadow of pollution havens did emerge in the newly industrialized economies of the Republic of Korea, Taiwan, Singapore and Hong Kong (Mani and Wheeler 1997). Subsequently, mainland China and other East Asian developing countries had a similar experience. The import-export ratio in these industries declined sharply, as the proportion of export of these dirty products increased. This phenomenon, however, was seen to be short-lived as the import-export ratios stabilized at ratios greater than unity, and these countries remain net importers of pollution-intensive products from developed countries. This phenomenon is explained by the increase in environmental regulations in the developing countries accompanying economic growth. Similarly, for the South Asian countries, including India, Pakistan and Bangladesh, the share of dirty industries in production continued to increase through the 1970s, but the region remained a net importer of pollution-intensive products (ibid: 26).

Another study on the pollution content of exports relative to imports[8] in India estimated that pollution content ratio increased from 0.29 in 1985 to 0.47 in 1992 and then marginally declined to 0.41 in 1996 (Banerjee and Chattopadhyay 2001). Similarly, the ratio of Indian exports to imports of relatively pollution-intensive products also increased between 1985 and 1992 from 0.12 to 0.19, and then registered a marginal decline to 0.188 in 1996 (ibid). On the other hand, the ratio of exports to imports of relatively cleaner products increased from 0.937 in 1985 to 1.79 in 1992, and then declined to 1.30 in 1996. The authors observed that while the late 1980s experienced gradual liberalization in India, the 1990s saw more open trade with enforcement of more rigid environmental regulations in the world economy, and this may have induced the estimated decline in pollution content of trade in India too.

This section will analyze the export of industrial manufactures in India to discern the trend observed in the trade of pollution-intensive products over the last three decades, and especially in the post-liberalization era. The structure of Indian exports has changed substantially over the long term, with the share of primary products declining and that of manufactured goods increasing in the total export basket. The share of primary products in total commodity exports declined from 37% in 1980-81 to about 24% in 1990-91. In contrast, the share of manufactured goods exports showed a persistent rise from 56% in 1980-81 to more than 70% by 1990-91 (*Reserve Bank of India*). The structural shift in the composition of India's exports continued through the 1990s, and in 2000-01, primary products contributed to 16% of total commodity exports, and the share of manufactured goods increased to 77% of commodity exports.

Within the primary goods sector, there has been a fall in the relative share of traditional agricultural exports of tea, tobacco, cashew kernels, spices and oil-cakes. On the other hand, exports of rice, fish and fish preparations, meat and meat preparations, vegetables, fruits, floricultural products and processed items have now become significant since the 1980s. Similarly, in the manufactured goods sector, non-traditional items such as gems and jewelry, engineering goods, ready-made garments, chemicals and allied products since the 1980s have overtaken traditional exports such as jute manufactures.

Although the relative significance of agriculture and allied products has declined, it continues to constitute a substantial part of total Indian commodity exports. This sector is particularly important, since it is the largest provider of employment to the phenomenal Indian population by specializing in say, processed and semi-processed foods. While the agri-sector holds export growth potential for developing countries like India, it is heavily protected by environmental and safety measures in developed countries.

Within the manufactured good sector, exports of textiles/garments are important, and in 2000-01 contributed to 23.5% of total commodity exports (based on RBI data). The textile and clothing industry accounts for about 20% of India's industrial output, and is the second largest employment provider. This sector too has been facing import restrictions based on environmental standards in OECD countries.

The threat of trade restrictions on environmental and health grounds against Indian exports most significantly come from three provisions in the multilateral trading system. First, the GATT Article XX exceptions under paragraphs b, d and g; second, the Agreement on Technical Barriers to Trade (TBT) covering technical regulations, packaging and ecolabelling; and third, The Agreement on The Application of Sanitary and Phytosanitary Measures (SPS) covering food safety and quality standards. As mentioned in Chapter 3, these provisions cover environmental and quality aspects of processes and production methods, including those unrelated to the characteristics of the end-product. The threat of future restrictions from these provisions is increasing with the steady growth in environmental trade notifications by member countries under the WTO since 1995.[9]

The major destination markets of Indian exports continue to be in the industrialized countries of the EU, Japan and the US. This group of countries absorbs more than half the commodity exports of India, and is also among the countries with the most stringent environmental standards (some stricter than international norms). Thus keeping up with environmental market challenges of these countries is important for Indian exporters.

4.3.1 Structure of Indian Manufactured Export

One way to discern any trade specialization trend in polluting industries is to track the performance of key Indian manufactured exports by sector. This section analyzes the performance by rank ordering the Indian merchandise at the sectoral level, and also the import-export ratios for traditional polluting products. The agricultural and allied sectors being relatively cleaner (also India does not export natural resources like timber which exacerbate resource degradation like deforestation) are not considered here.[10]

Six categories of manufactured exports stand out as being the most significant in value terms of the Indian manufactured export basket. These include: handicrafts, engineering goods, garments, textiles, chemicals and leather. The value contribution of this group of six manufactures has been steadily increasing in the last three decades, and during 1990-2001 contributed to more than 90% of total manufactured exports.

Table 4.5   The Six Significant Indian Manufactured Exports, 1990-2001
(Percentage share in total manufactured exports)

Commodity group	70-71[a]	80-81[a]	90-91	99-00	00-01[b]
1. Handicrafts	6.0	19.4	26.4	29.2	24.6
2. Engineering goods	13.7	18.0	17.3	17.3	19.9
3. Ready-made garments	3.7	14.3	17.2	16.0	16.1
4. Textile yarn, fabrics, made-ups	16.3	8.3	11.8	14.1	14.3
5. Chemical and allied products	4.5	5.9	10.0	11.5	11.7
6. Leather/ leather manufactures	10.3	9.5	11.5	5.4	5.6
Share in total manufactured exports	*54.5*	*75.4*	*94.2*	*93.5*	*92.2*

[a]   The classifications of commodity exports in 1970-71 and 1980-81 are not exactly comparable to 1990-91 and 2000-01 (the latter two years have same product categories). Thus for the sake of comparison, for the years 1970-71 and 1980-81, metal manufactures, machinery and transport equipment have been aggregated under Engineering goods.
[b]   Based on provisional export data for 2000-01.

Source: Author's calculations based on data in Table 117, RBI (2001).

In the last ten years, the rank order of the top four manufactured export product groups of India has remained unchanged, whereas, the fifth and sixth rank orders have been switched between the two sectors of leather manufactures and chemical-allied products. At the turn of the century, the top six manufacturing export sectors of India, in order, included: handicrafts, engineering goods, ready-made garments, textiles, chemicals and allied products and leather/leather manufactures. Table 4.5 lists the top six manufactured exports from India in 2000, and compares the share of these commodities in 1970, 1980 and 1990.

In 1970-71, jute manufactures constituted by far the single largest merchandise export from India, with a share of 23.3%, followed by textiles, iron and steel (under "Engineering" in Table 4.5), and gems and precious stones (under "Handicrafts" in Table 4.5). However, exports of jute manufactures declined dramatically over the last two decades in absolute value as well as in relative share, constituting less than 1% of manufactured exports during 1990-2000 compared to 8.3% in 1980-81 and 23.3% in 1970-71.

In 1980-81, the product group of "gems and precious stones" was the single largest export earner, followed by garments, machinery and transport equipment (under "Engineering"), and jute manufactures. Today gems and jewelry are categorized under the product group of handicrafts (a "clean" sector), and continues to be the highest export-earning industry by gross dollar value consistently since 1977. The share of handicraft exports increased steadily in the 1970s and 1980s, and by 1990-91 constituted 26% of manufactured exports. In the decade of the 1990s, the share has been in the range of 24-29%.

Another "clean" industry, namely ready-made garments, has also been expanding since the 1970s, and constituted about 15-17% of manufactured exports in the last decade. The textiles export sector (somewhat polluting) picked up in the late 1980s, particularly that of cotton textiles. The textile industry's pollution problem particularly stems from the use of chemical dyestuff. However, the last decade has increasingly seen the rise of eco-friendly textiles through certifications like Oko-Tex (discussed in chapter 6 under domestic firm behavior) and a renewed demand for traditional natural dyes in India.

The share of engineering goods exports has generally been increasing since the 1970s, except during 1983-87. Through the 1990s, engineering goods maintained a share of 17-20% of total manufacturing exports. The exports in this sector largely include machinery and equipment. India, however, still imports capital goods including manufactures of metals, machine tools, machinery, and electronic goods. The ratio of capital goods imports to engineering goods has been declining over the years from 4.4 in 1987-88 to 2.59 in 1990-91, and then to 1.74 in 1999-2000, indicating India's increasing specialization in this sector. However, since the import-export ratio is still greater than 1, India remains a net importer for engineering goods.

Based on the emission intensity of air pollutants, water pollutants and heavy metals, the five cleanest sectors include: textiles, non-electrical machinery, electrical machinery, transport equipment and instruments (Mani and Wheeler 1997: 5). Thus the trend of export expansion in the top four manufacturing sectors in India discussed above seem to be in relatively cleaner sectors of the industrializing economy of India.

The next two product groups of leather and chemicals (fifth and sixth in rank order), however, fall under the traditional "dirty" industries. The export performances of the two manufactures have been distinct. The share of leather manufactures, where the treating process involves extremely toxic chemicals, has declined from around 10% in the 1970s and 1980s to 5.6% in 2000-01. This sector, in particular, has come under increasing environmental scrutiny, both through standards in Western European countries (see chapter 6, which discusses how environmental regulations on toxic chemicals in OECD countries induced process changes in Indian tanneries in the 1990s), and domestic judicial activism. Indian Supreme Court rulings on leather industries in 1996 ordered tanneries to reduce pollution (see chapter 7 for details).

On the other hand, exports of chemicals and allied products have registered steady growth over the decades. The share of chemical and allied products has increased from barely 5% of total manufactured exports in the 1970s to about 12% in 2000-01. Within the chemical industry, however, a distinction is made between drugs, pharmaceuticals and fine chemicals, versus heavy industrial chemicals like dyeing, tanning, coloring materials, etc. The heavy chemicals are relatively more polluting than the finer chemicals.[11]

4.3.1.1 The Case of Export Specialization in Chemicals

Indian exports of both fine and heavy chemicals have increased over the last three decades; however, the composition of the chemical exports is biased towards the heavy chemicals. In 1970-71, the value of fine and heavy chemical exports were both around US$20 million, but the figures increased to $104 million and $171 million respectively in 1980-81, then further to $565 million and $741million in 1990-91 respectively, and to $1911 million and $2125 million in 2000-01. In other words, on the whole chemical exports have witnessed remarkable growth in both absolute and relative terms, and that of heavy chemicals has been more pronounced.

Table 4.6 Import-Export Ratio of Chemical and Allied Products, 1970-2001

Product group\ Year	70-71	75-76	80-81	86-87	90-91	95-96	99-00	00-01
Chemical and allied products	5.288	8.383	5.625	2.143	1.785	1.949	1.373	0.887
Of which								
Fine chemicals[a]	2.866	1.639	1.255	0.514	0.462	0.398	0.224	0.195
Heavy chemicals[b]	6.024	12.411	7.381	3.568	2.793	3.129	2.474	1.509

[a] Includes medicinal and pharmaceutical products.
[b] Includes organic and inorganic chemicals as well as fertilizers.

Source: Author's calculations based on export and import data in RBI (2001) Tables 117 and 119.

To illustrate the structural change in chemical trade in India, and the trend of specialization in this dirty sector, Table 4.6 shows the import-export ratio of this sector in general and for fine and heavy chemicals in particular, for the period 1970-2001. The import-export ratio of chemicals as a whole has fallen consistently since 1975 from 8 to less than 1 in 2000-01 (based on provisional data for 2000-01). Thus from a net importer India has now emerged as a net exporter of chemical and allied products, and fine chemicals. In heavy chemicals, the country still remains a net importer, but the emerging trend in specialization may soon change that. It is important to note, however, that the trend in the dirty sector is not unique to the post-liberalization era, but has been continuing since the 1970s.

Thus the trend in increasing exports of engineering goods as well as chemicals is closely linked to India's industrialization process, which has perhaps been accentuated by global market demand.

4.3.2 Pattern of Agricultural and Allied Exports

The nature of global food demand has changed over the last three decades towards more processed items, and this has been accompanied by stringent regulations in industrialized countries, and there have also been repeated rejections of export consignments from developing countries like India. The significance of credible food certification and conformity tests of exports has thus increased. The most important agricultural and allied export items from India include: marine products, rice, tea, spices, cashew, meat, coffee, processed fruits and vegetables. The implementation of stringent health and safety codes in the OECD countries has driven both institutional and structural changes within India.

The concern for food quality and safety has been increasing since there has been a marked shift in the type of food traded globally from mainly bulk raw materials to semi-processed and ready-to-eat food (value-added) products. Safety and quality aspects include microbiological contamination, hazard control, pesticide and drug residue in food, genetically modified content, export certification and international standard certification/individual country approval (like EU specific standards). Since mere physical inspection is not enough to detect potential hazards in food, the world trade in food products is largely guided by certification of both product and process. These standards ensure the safety of food products (e.g. chemical or genetic composition within permissible limits)[12] and minimize the health hazard by ensuring that the processing units operate under hygienic conditions (to reduce microbial contamination).

The export value of agricultural and allied products in India increased from US$3.2 billion in 1991-92 to US$5.9 billion in 2000-01 (DOC 2002). The significance of this sector has been declining as a proportion of total commodity exports; specific food products like marine products continue to be a high foreign exchange earner. In particular, marine/seafood exports constitute more than 3% of total Indian commodity exports and are categorized by the Department of Commerce as a high export-share product sector with growth potential (ibid). Marine products constituted almost a fifth of the total exports of agricultural and allied products during 1990-2000, followed by rice (see Table 4.7).

Other significant food export products include tea, coffee, spices, processed foods, meat, and fruits and vegetables. Indeed, food products like processed fruits and vegetables have been identified as sectors with untapped export potential (EXIM 2002). Thus, implementations of food safety and quality standards have become significant to maintain and expand global food markets for India.

In the 1960s, Indian fish exports were mainly in the form of dried fish, and in the 1970s and 1980s, fish exports were either canned or frozen. Today, in keeping with the worldwide trend in fresh and processed fish trade, Indian exports consist of fresh frozen and cooked frozen products (mostly shrimps). Thus food safety standards and HACCP (Hazard Analysis Critical Control Point) implementation in seafood processing facilities have become essential for Indian exporters to retain and expand markets abroad.

Table 4.7 Agricultural and Allied Exports during 1990-2000

Commodity	Total Exports (US $ million)	% Share in total
Marine Products	9230.1	18.78
Rice	7075.3	14.39
Oil Meals	6010.4	12.23
Tea	4170.9	8.48
Cashew incl. cashew nut shell liquid	3580.1	7.28
Coffee	2963.8	6.03
Spices	2544.6	5.18
Tobacco	1740.2	3.54
Cotton Raw including Waste	1703.2	3.46
Processed items incl fruits, juices etc	1592.6	3.24
Meat and Meat Preparations	1479.4	3.01
Fruits and Vegetables	1395.8	2.84
Sugar and Molasses	822.1	1.67
Others	4851.1	9.87
Total	*49159.6*	*100.00*

Source: Calculated from data in Table 117: Exports of Principal Commodities, RBI (2001).

In the 1990s, fishery products emerged as the dominant food item in value terms. In 2000-01, exports of Indian marine products earned a revenue of US$1.4 billion, accounting for more than 20% of the total exports of agricultural and allied products. The OECD countries as a group are the major importers (in value terms) of Indian food products: for seafood exports Japan is the single largest country destination followed by the US; in spices the US is the single largest importer followed by the EU member countries; and in tea and coffee the EU member countries are the major importers (besides Russia). While rice exports to the UK and the US is significant, most of India's rice exports go to the Middle East (particularly Saudi Arabia). However, value added food exports from India find the largest markets in developed countries, and the food processing industry is considered as one of the sunrise industries in the country.

Since the American, Western European and Japanese markets are the most important export markets, stringent quality and safety standards in these countries have adversely affected Indian food exports due to consignment rejections or outright bans in these markets. While the first shock in marine exports was felt in 1997, when the EU banned seafood imports from India due to sub-standard processing units, other food products have also faced import barriers in the US and EU (and to a lesser extent in Japan). In June 2001, the Indian Commerce Ministry noted that non-tariff measures/barriers (TBT and SPS measures) have adversely affected the Indian exports of fresh fruits, coffee, meat, rice and even herbal medicines. The measures included stipulations on labeling, chemical pesticide residue, bacteria, filth, and presence of genetically modified organisms.

Table 4.8   Number of Indian Food Export Consignments Refused by USFDA, 2001- 2002

Reason for Refusal / Food Category	Fish	Spices	Fruits	Rice	Others	Total Refusals	% refused
1. Filthy &/or insanitary	34	8	10	28	56	136	29.6
2. Filthy and salmonella	53	45	-	-	-	98	21.4
3. Labeling	-	11	4	-	58	73	15.9
4. Unsafe colour/ additive	-	2	4	-	40	46	10.0
5. Salmonella	11	26	-	-	1	38	8.3
6. Pesticide residue	-	3	14	-	9	26	5.7
7. Needs FCE and labelling	-	-	-	-	23	23	5.0
8. Filthy/ insan. & labelling	-	4	-	1	8	13	2.8
9. Aflatoxin	-	-	-	-	4	4	0.9
10. HACCP	2	-	-	-	-	2	0.4
Total refusals	100	99	32	29	199	459	100.0

Food Categories *Fish*: includes raw or cooked fish (but not fish pickles). *Spice*: includes fresh spices or processed spices. *Fruits*: fresh or processed fruits and vegetables, including dried tamarind. *Rice:* mostly Basmati rice. *Other:* pulses, pickles (including fish pickle), preserves, concentrates (including tamarind concentrate), jellies, papads, syrups, candies, etc.
Violation Codes of USFDA 1. *Filthy, insanitary, and or soaked wet*: Product consists of a filthy, putrid or decomposed substance or prepared/ packed or held under sanitary conditions/ contaminated with filth. 2. *Filthy and Salmonella*: Products refused on the basis of presence of filth and salmonella. 3. *Labeling:* Article violates labeling standards, including non-listing of ingredients or processing or firm/ manufacturer, or language used is not English. 4. *Unsafe color or additive*: Article seems to contain unsafe food additive or color. 5. *Salmonella*: Product appears to contain salmonella, a poisonous and deleterious substance injurious to health. 6. *Pesticide residue*: Article appears to be raw agricultural commodity or contains unsafe chemical pesticide. 7. *Needs FCE:* Manufacturer is not registered as low acid canned food or acidified food. 8. *Filthy and Labeling*: Products refused due to presence of filth and inadequacy in labeling. 9. *Aflatoxin*: Article appears to contain aflatoxin, a poisonous and deleterious substance. 10. *HACCP*: Failure of the importer to provide verification of compliance.

Source: Author's calculations based on data in various issues of *Monthly Import Refusal Report by Country* of the US FDA's OASIS (Operational and Administrative System for Import Support), August 2001 through July 2002.

In particular, during August 2001 through July 2002, the US Food and Drug Administration refused a total of 459 food export consignments from India. Several food products from India have been under automatic detention and testing in the US under the USFDA Automatic Import Alert since the 1990s (including basmati rice, farfar, fresh and frozen lobster/lobster heads, fresh raw/fresh frozen/cooked shrimp, morel mushroom, black pepper and sesame seeds). Table 4.8 gives the basis for refusal by category of food consignments from India.

The main cause of import refusals of Indian consignments by the USFDA is based on food contamination problems in the form of filth, insanitary or deleterious substances and/or salmonella, which accounted for 60% of all food consignment refusals during 2001-02 (see Table 4.8). However, issues related to labeling and additive violations have also emerged as an important basis for USFDA refusals. More than 36% of Indian consignments were refused on the basis of inadequate labeling of products, pesticide residue or unsafe additives.

To control the quality of Indian exports and pre-shipment inspection, the Export Inspection Council of India (set up under the Export Quality Control & Inspection Act, 1963) conducts consignment-wise inspection, in-process quality control, self-certification, and Food Safety Management Systems-based Certification (DOC Annual Report 2001-02). The Food Safety Management Systems-based certification, aligned with international standards on HACCP / Good Management Practices, is mandatory for fish and fishery products, egg products, and milk products (the latter was made mandatory in 2000). Moreover, as will be seen in chapter 6 later, the importance of food safety as well as quality has led to international certification of export food processing units in India, so as to ensure market access in the industrialized countries.

4.3.3 Emergence of a New Export Sector: Software Services

The growth of the Indian information and technology (IT) industry has been driven by the IT software services. The latter contributes to more than half the industry's total export revenue. Indeed, the software industry has been one of the fastest growing industries in India. Although the industry is still small compared to other traditional industries (say, textiles) accounting for about 2% of India's GDP, it is expected to account for over 7% of India's GDP by 2008 (Nasscom-McKinsey 2002).

The software services industry made a humble beginning more than two and a half decades ago in the mid-1970s. India's software industry has journeyed from being a virtual obscurity in the global market in the 1980s to a significant presence in the 1990s. The total software exports from India increased from less than US$5 million in 1980 to more than $9.5 billion in 2002-03, with more than 50% annual growth in export earnings during 1995 through 2001. Since 2001-02 the annual growth rate plummeted, mainly due to the slowdown in the US, which is the single largest importer of Indian software exports. The export growth rate is expected to pick up since Indian firms are focusing on value-added higher end services and aggressively signaling quality through certifications. Table 4.9 gives the value of software exports for the last seven years 1995-96 through 2001-02. The share of software exports to total exports from India has also been consistently increasing, from about 2% in 1995-96 to 14% in 2000-01!

Today the Indian software services industry is considered to be a mature sector with the largest software services exports among developing countries.[13] A number of factors have aided the growth of the IT export industry in India, with the most important being the availability of low-cost technically skilled labor. For foreign firms, this translated into significant cost savings through off-shore service provision and outsourcing to India. The second factor has been a large pool of English-speaking labor, and the time zone that made IT services from India convenient. Other strong enabling factors that helped in the take-off of this sector were the policies adopted by the central and some state governments to encourage industry development and exports. The government had already encouraged the development of software technology parks to boost, and provide incentives to the sector. Perhaps it is the concurrence of all these factors, coupled with the foresight of the Indian entrepreneurs and some government support, that is responsible for the astounding journey that this industry witnessed in the global market. The liberalization policy worked well since the required intellectual capital in the Indian IT industry was waiting to be tapped at a competitive cost.

The pattern of IT industry exports has changed over the years. While the Indian firms began with an emphasis on body-shopping, where movement of workers overseas at the client's site had been important, the pattern of software exports has changed over the years with offshore services increasing. In 1991-92, the share of offshore services was barely 5%, with on-site services accounting for 95% of software exports. According to the National Association of Software and Service Companies (Nasscom) in India, by the year 2000-01 offshore services increased to about 44% (on-site services declined to 56%) of software export revenues.

Table 4.9 Indian Software Services Export Growth, 1995-2001

Year	Year-on-year annual export revenue growth (%)
1995-96	53
1996-97	47
1997-98	60
1998-99	49
1999-2000	53
2000-01	57
2001-02	13

Source: Reserve Bank of India *Annual Report*, various years.

The success of the IT industry is partly attributable to the reputation that had been established in the global market, a feature unique to India as compared to some other Asian developing countries. To signal the quality and reliability of the IT services, Indian export firms have aggressively pursued international quality certification, particularly the Software Engineering Institute's Capability Maturity

Model (CMM) and more recently CMMi (Capability Maturity Model integrated), certified quality analyst, Six Sigma, etc. Software quality certification has emerged as one clear strategy of the Indian software export firms to keep ahead of the competition from software firms in other Asian developing countries (like China, and the Philippines) who have similar labor cost advantages.

Indian software exports have a large customer base of Fortune 500 companies. While software services are exported to about 100 countries around the world, the US dominates regional destination, accounting for a share more than half the total, followed by Europe. Thus the behavior of the Indian software services industry is largely determined by the global market, in particular that of the US. Not surprisingly, the slowdown in the US economy has been reflected in the deceleration in the growth of the industry in India during the last two years.

The industry has developed specialization and maturity in offshore delivery of services, with experience in handling large project implementation. Recently, Indian companies have also made modest headway in segments such as packaged software support and installation, product development and design services and embedded software solutions. More importantly the software industry has a reputation for high quality and reliability through a track record of on-time delivery. Indeed, according to Nasscom, one in every four global giants outsource their software requirements to Indian companies.

4.4 Conclusion

Thus, the post liberalization era in India has seen the expansion of exports in both relatively clean as well as dirty industries. The emergence of a clean export sector of IT services has been the most phenomenal experience in the post-liberalization period. Traditional clean sectors of handicrafts, ready-made garments, textiles and engineering goods continue to be significant export products. This has been accompanied by declining exports from the "dirty" leather industry. The one disturbing feature is the increasing specialization in the "dirty" sector of chemical and allied products, which has been continuing since the late 1970s. The growth of this "dirty" sector, however, is closely linked to India's industrialization process and not driven by exports per se.

Notes

[1] Out of the total approved FDI of approximately $71 billion during 1991-July 2001, approvals from the US constituted nearly $15 billion. Total FDI inflow to India during the same period was approximately $19 billion of which $3 billion came from investors in the US.

[2] To curb tax evasion, the tax department in India had served notices to various Mauritius based FIIs in March 2000 for payment of tax on capital gains and dividends, on the grounds that FIIs did not have effective management in Mauritius. In May 2002, the Delhi High Court ruled that a mere certificate of proof of FIIs residence in Mauritius

would not be sufficient to take advantage of the treaty. "Clear and Present Danger", *Economic Times* June 15, 2002: page 5.

3   *US-India Economic Relations*, November 2001.

4   USDOC 2001.

5   The prospects in this sector seem to have been enhanced since, for the year 2002, the Environment sector had been ranked sixth after sectors like Computer Software and Services, Telecommunication Services, Telecommunication Equipment, Computers and Peripherals, Education.

6   Of course the situation in the pre-liberalization era was worse: the regulatory restrictions (e.g. licensing and foreign exchange regulations) that reduced the likelihood of new foreign investment in India also eliminated the potential technological threat from international competitors (Athreye and Kapoor 2001: 417). Thus the incumbent foreign firms could continue to use technologies that were internationally obsolete (even if better than those of the domestic firms).

7   Conducted by the Centre of Science and Environment under the *Green Rating Project.*

8   Polluting industries were defined as those where abatement costs are close to 1% or more of the total value of output, and the study used pollution abatement costs of US industries to make the categorization.

9   For instance, according to the WTO Environmental Database 2000, the number of SPS notifications increased by 59% during 1997-2000 from 300 to 468; and those of environment-related notifications under TBT more than doubled from 41 to 97 during 1995-2000.

10   Food processing industries, which lead to organic water pollution (in terms of biological oxygen demand or BOD) are not considered here, although the food processing industry has begun to grow in recent years and may become a major polluting Indian industry. Pollution from the manufacturing industries has been the major focus of pollution control boards in India.

11   Industrial chemicals were identified as a pollution-intensive industry in Mani and Wheeler 1997: 4.

12   For example, aquaculture uses some chemicals that are considered to be highly hazardous to human health including chloramphenicol, organotin molluscicides, nalachite green and some organophosphates. These residues in seafood pose a risk to consumers through hypersensitivity to drug residues or the emergence of antibacterial-resistant intestinal microflora. (FAO 1997: 4)

13   Other developing countries, in particular the Philippines and China, are also aspiring to boost the software services industry to ride the global IT wave and replicate the Indian Silicon Valley phenomenon.

Chapter 5

The Consumption Effect

5.1 Sustainable Consumption

The consumption pattern of a society drives the production systems of the economy through the demand generated for different types of goods and services. The previous two chapters covered the government, trade and industry behavior in the post-liberalization period in India that have had significant environmental implications. The market economy, however, is driven by consumer behavior. Of course, the producers do play a role in influencing consumer preferences through advertising that can influence consumer psychology, which finally dictates the resource demands placed through the consumption of goods and services. In India the domestic market continues to play a major role, both in terms of the growth in traditional polluting industries and in terms of attracting foreign investment in industries with robust domestic growth. Thus consumption pattern of Indians today is a significant and integral component of the process of sustainable development.

While it is important to emphasize resource efficiency and pollution prevention in production, it is also important that the total consumption demand for resources from the ecosystem can be sustained for years to come. The definition of sustainable development, widely accepted today, is that path of economic growth where future generations have economic opportunities that are at least as large as that of the present generation.[1] The capacity to produce and consume goods and services depends on the capital assets of the economy: natural, manufactured and human capital. Natural capital consists of natural assets of the biosphere that supports all life forms, and the economic contributions include production of food, energy, air, water, minerals, habitat and biological diversity. Manufactured capital with the aid of human capital builds on natural capital. Thus while maximizing the current human welfare, it is essential to honor the natural capital constraint for sustainability of humanity.

Over the years, the resource intensity of output has improved in industrialized countries, as is evident from the decline in total material used per unit of gross domestic product (GDP); however, another trend has more than offset the resource efficiency gains, namely the increase in consumption. Some of these efficiency gains have been offset by *rebound effects* where improvements in efficiency become a stimulus for increased consumption (UNEP 2002). For example, automobile fuel efficiency increased significantly in the 1990s, but so did the passenger miles traveled, as income saved on motor fuel is spent on traveling more miles or on other forms of transport. In effect, as the total GDP has grown faster than the improvement in resource/energy efficiency, there has been a net increase in total resource use.

The first major challenge to the phenomenon of increasing stress on the environment through our conventional measures of welfare and quality of life, in terms of increase in GDP per capita, was sounded in *The Limits to Growth* (Meadows et al 1972). The book raised fundamental questions on resource depletion, pollution and the capacity of the ecosystem to absorb the type of development experienced around the world. The authors challenged (based on a computer simulation of existing behavioral pattern) that, if the present growth trends in world population, industrialization, pollution, food production, and resource depletion continued unchanged, the limits to growth on this planet will be reached sometime within the next 100 years. They felt that there was an urgent need to alter the growth trends and to establish a condition of ecological and economic stability sustainable far into the future. To this end, the book gave a call to design a new global equilibrium where society would be materially sufficient, socially equitable, and ecologically sustainable, and there would be a distinct move away from obsession with economic growth as measured conventionally.

In the following two decades, there were concerted efforts to upgrade technology and to evolve concepts and institutions to support a sustainable future for humanity. In 1992, the authors in a new work (Meadows et al 1992, *Beyond the Limits*) observed that, in spite of the world's improved technologies, greater awareness and stronger environment policies, many resource and pollution flows had grown beyond their sustainable limits.[2] To ensure sustainability, a two-pronged approach was suggested: first, a comprehensive revision of policies and practices that have perpetuated growth in material consumption and in population; second, rapid increase in the efficiency with which materials and energy are used. The system, of course, could be complemented with environmental protection and conservation policies.

In 1992, the Agenda 21 (in particular Principle 8, Chapter 4) adopted by nations,[3] observed that to achieve sustainable development and a higher quality of life for all people, unsustainable patterns of production and consumption have to be eliminated (along with appropriate demographic policies). In particular, promoting sustainable consumption in the development process is important for a large country like India:

> Developing countries should seek to achieve sustainable consumption patterns in their development process, guaranteeing the provision of basic needs for the poor, while avoiding those unsustainable patterns, particularly in industrialized countries, generally recognized as unduly hazardous to the environment, inefficient and wasteful, in their development processes.
>
> *(Agenda 21, Chapter 4, paragraph 8)*

The problem of unsustainability arises from the fact that extravagant and wasteful consumption of goods and services, no matter how efficiently produced, imposes a negative externality on others by limiting the resources left for them (considering the given endowment of natural capital). The member states at the 1992 Rio Conference were encouraged to analyze the consumption patterns in their countries in order to establish the impact of consumption patterns on the environment, as well as to identify balanced patterns of consumption worldwide, which the Earth can support in the long term. It was felt that all stakeholders, including government, industry and other agencies could reinforce the values that would encourage the sustainable pattern of consumption in the different countries. While emphasis on resource efficiency and environmental protection has continued during the last three decades, the issue of sustainable consumption has remained in the back seat.

By the end of the last century, about 20% of the global population living in the industrialized countries accounted for 86% of private consumption expenditures, while the poorest 20% living in developing countries accounted for a little over 1% (UNDP 1998:2). This raised serious concerns of sustainable consumption, since if the present day trend in consumption patterns were to be continued, the future generations would inherit the inequity and an over-stressed ecosystem.

More importantly, happiness from consumption, the index of true well-being, has remained elusive in the face of runaway consumption of the more affluent. As Scitovsky (1976, 1986) noted, consumption is addictive and each luxury quickly becomes a necessity, and a new luxury must be found to increase relative well-being – that the happiness people derive from consumption is based on whether they consume more than their neighbors and more than they did in the past. Household studies in the US illustrated that income needed to fulfil consumption aspirations doubled between 1986 and 1994.[4] Yet, psychological surveys in diverse societies suggest that while the upper classes in any society may be more satisfied with their lives than the lower classes, they do not seem to be more satisfied than the upper classes of poorer countries, nor more satisfied than the previous generation of affluent classes (Durning 1992).[5]

The environmental costs of the high consumption class are staggering, as resource consumption (energy, minerals) and waste generation rise at phenomenal rates (chemical waste, carbon dioxide, and plastics). Durning (1992) analyzed the world by three consumption classes: high-income consumers, middle-income consumers, and under consumers. The consumption pattern of high-income consumers (1.1 billion in number) constituting 20% of the global population, is characterized by a diet of meat, packaged food and soft drinks, are transported by private cars and use throwaway materials. The middle-income consumers (numbering 3.3 billion), 60% of the global population, have a diet of grain and clean water, are transported by bicycles and buses, use durable materials, and have virtually no "luxury" items. The remaining 20% of the population are the under consumers (numbering 1.1 billion) with insufficient grain, unsafe water, no vehicular transport, and dependent on local biomass. In particular, the US accounting for barely 5% of the global population, accounts for 22% of fossil fuel consumption, 24% of carbon dioxide emissions, and 33% of paper and plastic use (ibid).

The majority of the Indian population, living in villages, falls in the third category of under consumers (biomass dependence is high, see next chapter for details), while the affluent in the urban areas are moving towards consumption patterns of the high consumers. Globalization and marketing of consumerism are pushing consumers to aspire towards the automated, throwaway lifestyle of the industrialized countries: a consumer culture that imposes tremendous resource strain, and the consequences on air, water and land resources seem forbidding and hence unsustainable!

Economic theory suggests that inefficiency in consumption (just as in production), can be corrected through correct pricing of goods and services, that which internalizes the environmental costs. However, optimality in consumption equilibrium may not be consistent with sustainability, since optimality can be based on a high discount rate for the future. Thus potentially there can be an infinite number of efficient time paths, but only some which can be sustainable, given the initial endowments.[6] The pursuit of sustainable consumption (in pursuit of sustainable development), then needs to go beyond the pricing structure of goods and services (including environmental amenities directly consumed) to the very formulation of consumer preferences.[7]

In 1998, a workshop on Consumption in a Sustainable World in Norway identified that the most important social drivers and behavioral mechanisms are the media and information technology, the influence of the middle class, and the role of women in shaping patterns of consumption. To move towards sustainable consumption, there was a need to understand the relationship between globalization, equitable sharing and improved efficiency in the use of resources. In 2002, at the Johannesburg Summit, sustainable consumption was defined as a consumer movement away from consuming more and more products to satisfying needs with products that are fewer in number and are less environment- and resource-intensive.

Several options to relieve consumption pressures have been suggested in the literature, including: the use of improved technologies that come from the discovery of new knowledge; and shifts in lifestyle that lead to a more equitable sharing of the environment and social systems. In India, the processes of development and urbanization have brought about major changes in lifestyles. Greater global communication and aspirations for better quality of life, typically based on the consumption basket of an average citizen in a developed country like the US, have also resulted in changes in the preference patterns of domestic consumers.

5.2 Consumption and the Environment

The consumption of goods and services provides satisfaction and hence is the basis of the individual's (and society's) quality of life. Total consumption and the pattern of consumption have direct environmental impact through: first, the resource intensity of the goods and services consumed; and second, the wastes generated from the consumption. Thirty years ago, *The Limits to Growth* had raised doubts about the world's capacity to grow at the existing rate given the natural resource constraint (Meadows et al 1972), and technology provided a solution to achieve more with less. The concerns today have accentuated and revived these questions and it is recognized that human consumption and associated waste generation cannot continue as dictated by the conventional sense of well-being of simply "more is better".

While resource-saving techniques help produce more goods and services with less inputs, finally it is the pattern of consumption (driving production in the system) that determines sustainability of the development process. In the 2002 World Summit on Sustainable Development in Johannesburg, one of the major concerns observed was the growing disparity in levels of consumption between the rich and the poor countries, as well as within the developing countries. The current inequality in consumption between countries is so wide, that there is concern about the fundamental distortion that exists in the progress towards sustainable development (UNEP 2002). By the end of the twentieth century, the overall consumption of the richest 20% of the world's population was nine times that of the poorest 20% (ibid).

One measure that reflects the disparity in environmental stress of consumption across different groups is the measure of "ecological footprint": the amount of biologically productive space required in supporting the average consumer. Biologically productive areas include: cropland (for cultivation of food, fiber, rubber, etc), grazing land (for meat, milk, hides, etc); forests (for timber, fuel wood, wood fiber, and to sequester carbon dioxide); fisheries; and built-up areas (infrastructure for housing, transportation, industrial production).

Given that the disparity in resource intensity of consumption of the average citizen across countries is acute, the total ecological footprint of an industrialized country can be larger than that of a developing country, even though the population in the latter is several times that of the former. This is significant since population growth in developing countries is considered to be one of the main factors contributing to environmental degradation.[8] For instance, in 1999, the total ecological footprints of India and the US were 794.2 million hectares and 2,719.9 million hectares respectively, even though India's total population was more than four times that of the US. What really drives the difference in the total ecological costs of consumption between the two countries is the fact that the per capita ecological footprint of India (0.8 hectares/capita) is less than a tenth of that in the US!

The inequity across countries in consumption patterns reflects the extent to which industrialized countries have used the productive capacity of the ecological system. Effectively, this inequity leaves a small portion of the Earth's productive capacity for the growth of the developing countries, for humanity to remain within sustainable limits. For instance, an average American consumes 227 times as much petrol and 115 times as much paper as the average Indian! While the latter may not be of much consequence given the increased recycling of paper, the former is alarming given that energy resources are depletable (even if they are renewable, and more excavation is promised with improved technology).

In 1999, the total biologically productive land on the planet was estimated at 11.4 billion hectares, covering about a quarter of the Earth's surface (Wackernagel et al 2002). The world population being 5.9 billion, about 1.7 hectares of biologically productive land was available per person (assuming that 12% of nature is sufficient for maintaining biodiversity, *ibid*). The question remains as to how a high quality of life can be squeezed out of the available 1.7 hectares? Indeed, population growth and ecological deterioration will reduce this available area of 1.7 hectares per person over the years.

Most countries run a national ecological deficit, which indicates that the ecological footprint of the average consumer is greater than the available national biological capacity per capita. This is true not only for a developing country like India, with a national ecological deficit of 0.1 hectares/capita, but also true for developed nations like the US, Germany, Japan, the Netherlands, Singapore, etc.

The countries where the endowment of bio-capacity is much more per capita than their consumption stress, however, run ecological surplus, notably New Zealand, Canada, Brazil, Peru, Finland and Australia. Table 5.1 below gives the average ecological footprint of selected countries in 1999.

Table 5.1 The Ecological Footprints of Selected Nations, 1999

Country	Average ecological footprint (ha/ person)	Available bio-capacity (ha/ person)	Domestic ecological surplus (ha/ person)
Australia	7.6	14.6	7.0
China	1.5	1.0	-0.5
India	0.8	0.7	-0.1
Japan	4.8	0.7	-4.1
UK	5.3	1.6	-3.7
USA	9.7	5.3	-4.4

Source: Selected from data reported in Wackernagel et al (2002).

Consumer preference patterns and habits play a large role in the consumption patterns of people and nations, as is evident from the average ecological footprints of the different countries listed in the table above. The real concern is that if nations continue to pursue the current resource-intensive consumption path, it will reduce the Earth's capacity to support future life, i.e. jeopardize the process of sustainability. An equally discomforting feature is the increase in consumption disparity and ecological footprints between the rich and the poor within developing countries as the more affluent groups in developing countries like India try to mimic the consumption pattern of, say, an average American citizen.

5.3 Consumption with Urbanization

The consumption path of economies is largely affected by the degree of urbanization, since lifestyles undergo significant changes with city dwelling. Increased communication in the world economy tends to homogenize consumer taste patterns across the globe and an average consumption basket of developed countries tend to be the benchmark of well-being. This section highlights the trend in consumption with negative externality in India – namely that of private ownership of vehicles.

The typical Indian lifestyle appears frugal by the current average standards in developed countries, not merely due to poverty but also due to traditional consumption habits. However, this has been changing with increase in average income, urbanization (both being proxies for development) and globalization (leading to similar consumption aspirations across countries).

While urbanization is traditionally considered as an index of development, severe pollution problems are associated with the phenomenon – unless urbanization is planned well to incorporate ecological factors (e.g. ensure ample tree cover, minimize natural habitat destruction and loss of biodiversity). In India, urbanization has been steadily increasing, and today about 30% of the total population is urban, representing more than 300 million people (see Table 5.2).[9] Indeed, urban planning in India has consistently fallen short of the actual urban growth leading to severe environmental problems in the cities, including inadequate capacity to provide clean water or treat household water effluents, or collect and treat municipal solid waste.

Table 5.2 Population and Extent of Urbanization in India, 1981-2001

Variable \ Year	1981	1991	2001
Population (millions)	683	846	1027
Population density (persons/km^2)	216	267	324
Population growth rate % (average annual)	2.2	2.1	1.9
Urbanization (% of total population)	23.3	25.7	30.5

Source: Data compiled from *Census India 2001* and Ministry of Urban Affairs.

Rising per capita income and consumption in cities, coupled with high population densities, have increased the environmental stress. There has been a phenomenal increase in air pollution (primarily from vehicles), and waste generation in the cities. Poor infrastructure has led to the release of untreated wastes and sewage into the rivers and waterways. Although the sanitation facilities available to urban India are better than those of rural India (considering, in the year 2000, 73% of the urban population had access to improved sanitation facilities compared to 14% of the rural population), the environmental stress in cities is telling.

The change in consumption patterns in urban India is evident from the change in the composition of the waste generated. The characteristics of the urban waste generated depend on conditions like the food habits of the population, cultural as well as socio-economic factors and climatic conditions. The use of non-biodegradable substances as well as metals and glass has increased. Comparing the physio-chemical characteristics of urban solid waste generated in 1971 and 1995, it is seen that plastics, glass and metals increased dramatically (see Table 5.3). Of course, these substances are recyclable, and would in turn encourage the economic activity of recycling and recovery of wealth from waste. However, the total volume of waste generated has also been increasing and there are issues regarding the extent to which some materials can be recycled – i.e. it may not be economically feasible to recycle 100% of the waste generated and landfills will continue to be filled with the wastes not recycled.[10]

Table 5.3   Physio-chemical Characteristics of Urban Solid Waste in India (percentage of weight)

Component	1971-73	1995
Paper	4.14	5.78
Plastics	0.69	3.90
Metals	0.50	1.90
Glass	0.40	2.10
Rags	3.83	3.50
Ash and fine earth	49.20	40.30
Total compostable matter	41.24	41.80
Calorific value (kcal/kg)	800-1100	<1500

Source: State of the Environment, MOEF (2001).

Indeed, the experience of several industrialized countries has shown that with economic growth, there is no respite from increasing solid waste generation or air pollutants like carbon dioxide (World Bank 1992: 11). There exists a direct relationship between growth in per capita income and per capita municipal waste (or per capita carbon dioxide emissions since more energy, no matter how clean, is consumed), which reflects the fact that consumption becomes more resource- and energy-intense, at high levels of income.

The de-linking of economic growth and adverse environmental impact is evident only for select pollutants, like atmospheric sulfur dioxide, nitrogen oxides, and particulate matter. The inverted-U shaped environmental Kuznets curve illustrated that the environmental index for these pollutants increasingly deteriorates with increase in per capita income, hits a peak, and eventually reduces with further growth. Of course this is good news for a country like India where suspended particulate matter is a major threat to the health of the urban residents, and further economic growth promises to bring down the pollutant level. However, the increasing trend in vehicle consumption in India is unlikely to reduce the pollution load in the city air.

5.3.1 Income-Consumption Groups in India

In the post-liberalization period, both household income and consumption structure have witnessed significant changes, and there has been a more rapid movement of households towards higher income groups. A survey at the turn of the last century noted that large numbers of people in developing/emerging economies, approximately a total of 750 million, were entering the high consumption classes.[11] In India, about 80 million people were estimated to be part of the global consumer class, who share similar tastes and preferences in consumption.[12] The composition of the Indian income-consumption brackets has changed remarkably in the last two decades. The change reflects the increasing well-being of the entire population as a whole, as well as of sections of the population who have climbed up the income brackets. The proportion of the population in the low-income bracket declined from 65% in 1985-86 to 49% in 1995-96 and further to 42% in 1997-98 (see Table 5.4, listing the five income-consumption classes for the period 1985-98). There has been a relatively rapid movement of households towards higher income brackets. The absolute number of low-income households also declined (by 9.7 million during 1992-96 and by 8.6 million during 1995-98).

Table 5.4 Income-Consumption Groups* (percentage of population), 1985-1998

Income Class \ Year	1985-86	1992-93	1995-96	1997-98
Low	65.2	58.2	48.9	42.5
Urban	42.1	38.4	27.9	21.9
Rural	73.1	65.5	57.2	50.7
Lower middle	25.2	25.4	30.7	33.5
Urban	35.8	33.0	34.9	34.4
Rural	21.4	22.6	29.0	33.2
Middle	6.9	10.4	11.9	13.4
Urban	15.2	16.1	20.3	22.1
Rural	4.0	8.2	8.6	9.9
Upper middle	1.5	3.7	5.0	5.8
Urban	3.9	7.6	9.6	11.3
Rural	0.7	2.3	3.1	3.6
High	1.1	2.3	3.5	4.8
Urban	3.1	4.9	7.3	10.3
Rural	0.3	1.4	2.0	2.7

*The income consumption classes are based on annual income at 1997-98 prices: *Low* is less equal to Rs 30,000; *Lower middle* = Rs 30,001-60,000; *Middle* = Rs 60,001-90,000; *Upper middle* = Rs 90,001-125,000; *High* is income greater than Rs 125,000.
The three sets of numbers against each income class gives first the country-wide percentage of population in that class followed by the urban and rural figures.

Source: Selected from tables in Batra (2000).

In urban India, the upward mobility in income classes is more pronounced, both in terms of the decline in proportion of the population in the low-income group and growth of the high-income group: the proportion of urban households in the low-income bracket reduced from 38% in 1992-93 to 22% in 1997-98. The population in the high-income bracket increased from 3% in 1985-86 to 10% in 1997-98. Correspondingly, the ownership of durable consumer goods increased faster in the urban areas than in the rural areas, and the growth was more pronounced for consumer goods in the most expensive range (including color television, washing machines, video recorder and player, etc).[13] The new global consumer class in India consists of the urban population in the high-income and upper-middle-income brackets. Globalization has now made these consumers aspire towards consumption patterns observed in the developed countries, and not merely to doing better than before, or better than their immediate neighbors. In other words, greater information flow (as well as advertisement) is moving the affluent Indian class to conform to the global consumption class.

5.3.2 Vehicle Consumption in India

Vehicle ownership of a population often signifies the increase in well-being of the society, as well as the lack of a good mass transit system. On both counts, the ownership of consumer vehicles has increased in India. This in turn has aggravated the air pollution problem, especially in the cities, since increased consumption of vehicles per population has led to greater pollution emission per person (for the same distance traveled).

The growth of internal combustion vehicles in urban areas has been a global phenomenon and has led to: a rise in traffic congestion (hence more travel time); increased demand for oil; and deterioration of air quality (increased emissions of greenhouse gases, including carbon dioxide, methane, ozone, carbon monoxide, and nitrous oxide). For example, according to the World Resources Institute (WRI), worldwide, motor vehicles emit over 900 million metric tons of carbon dioxide each year, accounting for more than 15% of global fossil fuel carbon dioxide releases. High motor vehicle consumption in OECD countries contributed to two-thirds of total world carbon dioxide emissions in 1993, even though these countries represented only 16% of the world's population (WRI). At present, however, the per capita consumption of vehicles in India is still small, compared to industrialized countries like the US: there are about seven vehicles per 1000 persons in India, while by contrast, there are about 750 motor vehicles per 1,000 persons in the United States!

While liberalization has brought in newer and better car models in the domestic market at bargain prices,[14] mass transit systems in the cities remain poor. This has encouraged increased ownership of cars and two-wheelers in India increasing both road congestion and air pollution. Table 5.5 shows the phenomenal increase in vehicle population and the composition of the vehicle fleet in India during 1975-98. The proportion of two-wheelers in the total vehicle fleet has been consistently increasing from 38% in 1975 to 56% in 1985 and further to 69% in 1998. Two-wheelers being a more affordable private vehicle for the majority, the consumption has increased at a phenomenal rate. On the other hand, the proportion of buses (a proxy for public transport facility) reduced from 4% in 1975 to 2.4% in 1985 and further to 1% in 1998. Thus foreign investment in the transport sector has certainly not changed the trend, but has targeted the growing consumer vehicle sector (two-wheelers and cars).

The increase in vehicle consumption pattern at the national level is mirrored in the metropolitan cities. Table 5.5 gives the total vehicle registration and vehicle composition in all metropolitan cities in 1997, and for the four major metros. Two-wheelers and cars, which have increased dramatically over the last decade, comprise the bulk of the vehicle fleet ranging from 14% to 33% in the four major metros. On the other hand, buses, a proxy for public transport, constitute less than 2% of the total vehicle population in these cities. Thus, while economic growth in urban India has witnessed rising income and consumption, the increase in well-being is partly offset by the adverse health effects of increasing atmospheric pollution (i.e. higher income per capita accompanying higher emissions per capita).

Table 5.5 Total Registered Vehicles in India (in thousands) 1975-1998[a]

Vehicles/Year	1975	1980	1985	1990	1995	1998
All vehicles	2,472	4,521	9,170	19,152	30,259	40,939
Of which (% share):						
2- wheelers	38.3%	46.8%	56.5%	65.8%	68.8%	69.2%
Cars, jeeps, taxis	31.0%	23.4%	17.5%	14.1%	12.7%	12.4%
Buses	4.6%	3.1%	2.4%	1.6%	1.4%	1.3%
Others[b]	26.1%	26.7%	23.6%	18.5%	17.2%	17.1%

[a]Pertaining to March of respective years.
[b]includes three-wheelers, trucks, tractors, trailors etc.

Source: TERI Energy Data Directory and Yearbook 2001.

In the 1990s, the city of Delhi, followed by Bangalore, emerged as the epicenter of India's economic modernization.[15] The sudden spurt of investment, and employment generation (consequently urban population growth) in Delhi led to a disproportionate growth of vehicle population, without corresponding urban planning to accommodate the increased population in a sustainable manner. The increase in vehicle population and corresponding air pollution led Delhi to become the fourth most polluted city in the world in the early 1990s (besides being one of the most polluted Indian cities). Delhi has by far the highest vehicle registration among all metropolitan cities in India, and experienced the highest growth rate of motor vehicles, compared to the other metropolitan cities. In 1996-97, buses constituted less than 2% of Delhi's vehicle fleet (see Table 5.6), and the public transport system was complemented with taxis and auto rickshaws (three-wheelers) in lieu of an inadequate mass transit system.

The growth of vehicle consumption in India is a continuing trend from the previous decades due to the shortcomings of the public transport system. The existence of this distortion further encouraged the increase in private ownership of vehicles in the post-liberalization era, which made a large range of energy-efficient vehicles available to the Indian consumers. This has basically led to a trade-off between environmental gain per vehicle (due to the increased energy efficiency of consumer vehicles), and more pollution due to the increase in the total number of private vehicles (scale effect).

Besides imposing environmental pollution costs, this phenomenal increase of motor vehicles poses a strain on the total energy consumption (since petroleum imports account for more than half of India's bulk imports).[16] Moreover, while ownership of multiple vehicles for Indian consumers may seem to be a sign of well-being, the health and environmental costs of multi-car households are much higher than that in industrialized countries, given the poor air quality. Thus even though economic gains and market trends make car ownership more affordable, the rate of growth of vehicle registration in the Indian cities does not seem environmentally sustainable.

Table 5.6 Total Registered Vehicles in Metropolitan Cities, 1996-1997

Vehicles	Total	Delhi	Bangalore	Chennai	Mumbai
All vehicles	9,885,172	2,629, 646	972,373	889,819	796, 913
Of which (% share):					
2- wheelers	69.9%	66.2%	72.8%	73.4%	41.3%
Cars	16.2%	25.2%	14.4%	17.6%	32.6%
Buses	1.3%	1.1%	1.4%	0.6%	1.6%
Others*	12.6%	7.5%	11.4%	8.4%	24.5%

*includes three-wheelers, taxis, jeeps, trucks, tractors, trailors etc.

Source: Automeet-Autostatistics.

5.3.3 Defensive Environmental Expenditure

The poor environmental quality of air and water in Indian cities has led to an increase in defensive consumer expenditure, in order to avoid adverse health impact in the direct consumption of these natural resources. Gas masks are readily available in Indian stores and it is common to see city commuters and traffic police wearing these masks. The poor quality of drinking water has led to a dramatic growth in the market of packaged drinking water and water purification implements, especially since the 1990s.

The total domestic market for packaged waster in 2001 was estimated to be around US$140-200 million, with an annual growth rate of 40%.[17] During 1993 and 1997, the sale of bottled water alone increased more than 100-fold over the five years (CMIE 2000). This reflects the underlying demand for some of the essential environmental services from the domestic sector. It also clearly indicates that communities in urban India (except for the urban poor) are willing and do pay for improvement in environmental quality of the basic consumption goods and services. Thus, while the majority of Indians can ill-afford the cost of the full market price of basic resources like water and sanitation, a certain section of the Indian population, notably in the urban areas, can pay more for enhancing these services that follow from privatization and liberalization.

Besides defensive environmental expenditure, there are also shades of green-consumerism creeping into the upmarket department stores in Indian cities. While Indians have not yet embraced green-consumerism as understood in the OECD countries, the urban market has introduced "environmentally-friendly" television sets and refrigerators. Fabrics using natural dyes have also become popular, as have nature-based ayurvedic cosmetic and pharmaceutical products as consumers find merits in goods reviving traditional knowledge and heritage.

5.3.4 Striving towards Clean Consumption

Although pollution from production has been declining in developed countries and consumption patterns are considered to be getting greener, the environmental burden of the average citizen's consumption has been increasing in these countries as discussed earlier. In comparison, the environmental burden of consumption patterns in a developing country like India is relatively lower. However, if the Indian consumers, in a bid to be part of the global consumption class, strive for the average consumption basket of developed countries, then the economy would run into a severe resource crunch.

In the last decade, the ecological cost of consumption in Indian cities has been rising with an energy-intensive consumption pattern. The challenge ahead for the Indian urban society is to arrest the ecological strain, while increasing well-being. Sustainable consumption can be achieved through factors affecting consumer behavior, and goes beyond green-consumerism, since it would encompass the notion of ecological footprint.

Consumption patterns of any society depend on a host of factors, including community traditions and norms, demography, advertising, availability of information, etc. The traditional Indian lifestyle had close ties with ecological factors, and certain community practices had in-built natural resource preservation methods: for instance, in the state of Bengal where the staple is fish, traditionally the Bengalis did not consume certain species during the spawning period, to ensure re-generation of the species. However, changes in demography, social structures, lifestyles and urbanization have brought in major changes – even in food consumption. Today urban consumption does not follow seasonal food habits (even villages have lost the incentives dictating traditional behavior, like observing non-hunting seasons).

Worldwide urban communities have more meat in the diet than rural communities who consume more grains. This implies that urban consumption is more land intensive due to the feed required for animals. However, since the vast majority of Indians are vegetarian, this cultural factor may offset to some extent the same pattern for India. Similarly other cultural values of India can help evolve a new consumption path for the society, so that in the pursuit of well-being, the unsustainable patterns of consumption observed in industrialized countries are not replicated.

5.4 Culture to Lead Sustainable Consumption

Consumer preference theory in economics suggests that more may not always be better since consumers can hit a point of satiation.[18] However, with newer commodities and services being available, the domain of the consumer preference keeps increasing, and the satiation point is typically ignored. To gauge whether well-being has indeed increased with higher material consumption, psychological studies have attempted to map actual consumer satisfaction from the increased consumption experienced. Durning (1992) observed that runaway consumption does not seem to have made people much happier, and there is almost no difference in the levels of reported happiness found in the very wealthy and the very poor countries.

The studies suggest that material consumption has failed to fulfil the consumer society since social, psychological and spiritual hunger has remained in the society, and after all, happiness and well-being are derived not merely from material consumption but a host of other factors. Studies on happiness have indicated that the main determinants of happiness in life are not related to consumption at all, but include satisfaction with family life, especially marriage, followed by satisfaction with work, leisure to develop talents, and friendships. Moreover, the increase in consumer information regarding environmental impact of consumption can change the underlying preference pattern towards lower resource-intensive consumption. Therein lies the answer to the question Scitovsky (1986) raised almost two decades ago: can resource costs be reduced without reducing consumer satisfaction?

Since consumer happiness has not been found to be more in the developed countries than in the developing countries, where the differences in national consumption patterns are typically cultural and historical, there is a way to assimilate consumer values across nations to achieve the least resource-intensive consumption path. Indeed today the world has started to re-evaluate the role of traditional lifestyles and values, and create a "hybrid culture of consumption" (Robins 2000). While market signals can communicate the environmental implications of production and consumption, there is a growing consciousness that traditional values of lifestyles need to be reinforced. Such a lifestyle would combine eco-efficient technology in production with a traditional approach to nature and society in consumption. Robins holds an optimistic view on opportunity of sustainable consumption in developing countries, since the South has not yet invested in the physical infrastructure, technological capital and lifestyles that drive unsustainable consumption in the North! Even though market globalization and liberalization coupled with intensive communication links are harmonizing consumption patterns across the globe, there is still room for evolving a distinct path to sustainable consumption through existing cultural values in developing countries.

This is heartening given the fact that even today, the middle-class Indian population follows a relatively frugal lifestyle, if only by default of habit. The traditional Indian frugal approach to material consumption can be viewed as a distinct advantage in evolving a sustainable consumption path, without sacrificing increase in well-being. In other words, it is a comparative advantage in environmentally sustainable consumer preferences! Thus a new path of improving well-being can be defined by reinforcing cultural and traditional consumption values, much like the way traditional knowledge is being formally recognized as environmental wealth.

It is possible for the Indian urban society to achieve a unique sustainable consumption path by defining a lifestyle based on the wealth of traditional values and culture. In this regard, increasing environmental education and information, as well as formally recording the traditional knowledge (discussed in chapter 9) will help Indian society to evolve such a new path of consumption. A pattern of sustainable consumption in India is essential to ensure intra-generation equity (given the vast majority of under consumers), besides inter-generation equity (as required for sustainable development). Since consumption patterns have been seen to be more important than population in determining resource costs of an economy (comparing total ecological footprint of India with the US), India's billion plus population may even force a turnaround in its environmental Kuznets curve at a low per capita income level!

Notes

[1] Pearce and Barbier (2000).

[2] The authors also observed that: "Given some of the technologies and institutions invented over those twenty years, there are real possibilities for reducing the streams of resources consumed and pollutants generated by the human economy while increasing the quality of human life. It is even possible, we concluded, to eliminate poverty while accommodating the population growth already implicit in present population age structures – but not if population growth goes on indefinitely, not if it goes on for long, and not without rapid improvements in the efficiency of material and energy use and in the equity of material and energy distribution."

[3] Adopted by India in 1992.

[4] UNDP (1998): 60.

[5] Several consumer happiness surveys among Americans showed that while per capita income increased by 62% during 1946-70, the proportion of people who considered themselves very happy, fairly happy and not too happy had hardly changed in the 25-year period! Thus Scitovsky observed that even with the economic welfare rising, we are no happier as a result! (Scitovsky 1976: 134-35, quoting ten such surveys).

[6] See Pearce and Barbier (2000), Pearce and Warford (1993), Pezzey (1989) on the analysis of sustainability.

[7] The valuation of the environment based on the consumer's willingness to pay, for instance through contingent valuation, is an attempt to capture the consumer's altruism and conserve the environment for its sheer existence value (non-use value) and as a bequest to future generations.

[8] Others being poverty, lack of well-defined property rights, ecologically insensitive government growth policies, etc.

[9] Among the regions with greater urbanization are the union territories of Delhi (92.73%) and Chandigarh (93.63%), and the states of Maharashtra (38.73%) and Gujarat (34.4%). "*Urban Scenario*", Ministry of Urban Affairs, website http://urbanindia.nic.in.scene.htm.

[10] Urban solid waste includes household garbage and rubbish, street sweeping, construction and demolition debris, sanitation residues, as well as industrial and hospital solid wastes. Municipal solid waste covers all the above, which are not hazardous in nature. At present, the urban solid waste generated in India is largely dumped in landfill sites (which are typically not sanitary), with little being composted.
Recent regulatory initiatives have addressed the issue of urban solid wastes in India: according to the *Municipal Solid Wastes (Management and Handling) Rules 2000*, the urban development authorities are now responsible for identifying the landfill sites and handing over the sites to the concerned municipal authority for development, operation and maintenance. Hazardous and biomedical wastes management are covered by the Hazardous Wastes (Management and Handling) Rules 1989 (amended 2000) and the Bio-Medical Waste (Management and Handling) Rules 1998 respectively. The Amendment Hazardous Waste Management Rules in 2000, requires state governments or

the operators of facilities/associations to identify sites for disposal after conducting an Environmental Impact Analysis.

[11] UNEP (2002) quoting *Myers and Kent* (2000) *The New Consumers,* report to the Winslow Foundation, Washington D.C.

[12] Ibid.

[13] The rural ownership of durable goods (especially of the more expensive durable products) has also witnessed steady growth over the last decade. The continuing rural-urban difference in the penetration of expensive electrical durable consumer goods is explained mostly by infrastructure deficiencies like electricity and roads, followed by income level disparity between rural and urban households (Batra, 2000: 9-11).

[14] There has been a phenomenal increase in the range of consumer cars that have flooded the market in the post-liberalization era in India, and this has instilled competition in the car sector. For example, Maruti Udyog, which has been the market leader since the 1980s in the consumer car sector, was compelled to offer a wider range of fuel-efficient models in the 1990s as competition increased.

[15] More than half the MNCs that set up shop in India in the 1990s established their bases in Delhi.

[16] Based on the RBI data, crude petroleum and petroleum products have typically constituted a share of about 20 to 25% of India's total import bill in the 1990s.

[17] The total market in India is estimated to be in the range of Rs 700-1000 crores (Bhushan 2002).

[18] In theory, a satiation point is defined in the consumption space as that consumption bundle beyond which the consumer cannot enhance her/his happiness or utility from consumption. However, the domain of analysis has always been well within that space, since as the standard of consumption rises the satiation point has been pushed beyond the space of consideration.

Chapter 6

Emergence of the Indian Environment Market

6.1 The Global Environment Industry

The internalization of environmental costs in economic activities has led to the emergence of the environment industry. Growing environmental consciousness, increasing environmental regulations and standards, and the drive to increase resource efficiency has led to the development of pollution abatement technology and equipment, resource-efficient technologies and management practices, as well as environmental services in consulting, auditing, impact analysis, etc. Firms producing traditional products, ranging from engineering goods to textiles to food, have been projecting an environmentally friendly image to capture the market niche of environmentally conscious consumers.

The environment industry consists of three sectors in the environment market: equipment, services, and resources (*Environmental Business International Inc.*, based on the US Standard Industry Classification system). The total revenue generated under each sub-sector determines the size of the environment industry: equipment revenues are sales of hardware; services revenues pertain to fees paid for services like waste treatment, waste management, remedial services, consulting, engineering, testing and analytical services; and resources are sales of material, water or energy. The OECD and the Statistical Office of the European Commission (Eurostat) classification, on the other hand, includes "resources" under the services sector. In terms of environmental activities in this industry, the OECD/ Eurostat distinguishes three such groups: (a) pollution management group; (b) cleaner technologies and products group; and (c) resources management group.

The global environment industry (equipment, services, and resources) experienced rapid growth in the 1980s following increasing enforcement of environmental regulations and economic instruments in the industrialized countries (notably the US, Germany, France, the UK, and Japan). In the decade of the 1990s, however, the environment industry began to show signs of maturity and stagnation in these countries as the growth rates dropped sharply.[1] In particular, a study of the US environment industry noted that the maturity of the sector was heavily dependent on the demand by regulations, and thus in the 1990s the industry suffered from "waning regulation-induced market growth" (Berg and Ferrier 1998). In the developing countries including India, on the other hand, double-digit annual growth rates were experienced in the 1990s, especially since the stringency and scope of domestic environmental regulations began to increase. The environment market in developing countries of Africa, Asia and Latin America, which at present account for less than 10% of the worldwide market, is expected to grow at a rate of 10 to 15% per annum.

By the year 2000, the global environment industry was worth US$522 billion approximately. Industry surveys in the mid-1990s had estimated that the environment industry would increase to US$600 billion by 2010, with an average annual growth rate of 5% (WTO 1998). At present, the industrialized countries, namely the US, Western European countries and Japan, dominate the global environment industry, accounting for about 85% of the global market. The environment markets in these industrialized countries exhibited a robust growth in the 1980s, but the growth rate of the aggregate market dipped to a low of 2% to 3% per annum in the following decade.

In particular, the growth of the environment market in the US, which commands the largest share of about half the global market, dipped in the 1990s. The American environment market registered a growth of 28% during the 1990s, which was almost half of the growth during the 1970s and 1980s (Ferrier 2000). The median profit margins of US environmental firms exceeded 10% in the late 1980s, but ranged between 2% to 3% in the 1990s in the service segments (Berg and Ferrier 1998).

While the domestic environment markets in OECD countries reached saturation, exports from the environmental firms in these countries, especially those providing environmental services, became a significant growth factor. The export revenues of the environment industry constitute about 15-20% of the total output produced in Japan and Western European nations, and about 10% for the US industry. In the US, export revenue growth represented more than 50% of the growth of the US environment industry during 1996-97 (*Environmental Business International*). In particular, the American environment industry has turned the market focus on several Asian countries including India under the United States-Asia Environmental Partnership (US-AEP), given the growth prospects of these countries' domestic environment sectors.

There has also been a concerted effort within the multilateral trading system under the WTO to encourage free trade in environmental goods and services. The Doha Ministerial Declaration in November 2001, while reaffirming the WTO's commitment to support sustainable development through free trade, set down the agenda for future environment-trade negotiations (among others). In particular, Paragraph 31 (iii) of the Declaration indicated the mandate to reduce or eliminate tariff and non-tariff barriers to environmental goods and services through negotiations by the year 2005. The free trade in environmental goods and services under the WTO is likely to boost the global environment industry, especially with the increasing demand for clean technology and environmental management and remedial services in developing countries like India.

6.2 The Indian Environment Industry

The development of the Indian environment industry has closely followed the domestic regulation system and more recently the demands from international environmental statutes. The factors that have supported the rapid growth in this sector include rapid population growth and urbanization, industrialization, besides the enhanced domestic and international environmental regulations/provisions.

The infrastructure of environmental services (including sewage, sanitation, and solid waste management) in Indian cities have been unable to keep up with the rapid increase in population. This is particularly critical since the urban population is growing faster than the total population: during 1991-2001 the urban population increased by 32.26% while the country's total population increased by 21.34% during the same period.[2]

A second significant demand for environmental services comes from the industrial sector, particularly for industrial wastewater treatment and disposal hazardous waste management, upgrading environmental management systems, environmental analysis, consulting, testing and certification. The increase in the demand for environmental services in the industrial sector in India during the 1990s stems from three major factors, namely: enhanced domestic environmental regulations and initiatives, increasing demands for environmentally sound products from developed countries, and civil society pressure as well as environmental judicial activism.

Table 6.1 Investment Potential in the Indian Environment Sector, 1994
(in US$ million)

Environment Segment	Net Capital Investment Potential*
Waste Water Treatment	
Industrial	700.2
Municipal	660.0
Solid Waste Management	
Municipal (composting)	90.0
Industrial Hazardous	46.0
Industrial Non-Hazardous	n.a.
Other services	
Air Pollution	
Industrial	313.9
Mobile	40.0
Environmental Consultancy	38.0
Water and Air monitoring/ testing equipment & services	17.7
Total	1905.8

* Total estimated capital investment required in 1994 less the capital investment incurred.
n.a. => no information was available.

Source: Data from Table 4.1.1 in CII (1996).

The third potential demand for environmental services (for remedial services) comes from the need to clean up the present degraded state of the environment in the country. The indiscriminate disposal of untreated wastes and effluents into waterways and land has led to severe surface and ground water pollution. During the last five years in particular, the Ministry of Environment and Forests has more than doubled its expenditure on the environment to US$180 million in 2001-02, the largest outlay of $58 million being for cleaning up the rivers (MOEF 2002). Under the 1995 National River Conservation Directorate, remedial and pollution control works were undertaken for 18 major rivers in India.

The estimates of the current size of this environment market has a wide range between US$4 billion to US$8 billion, and includes the market of pollution control equipment as well as environmental consulting services.[3] The first comprehensive estimate of the Indian environment market including equipment and services was made for the year 1994 and was valued at US$1.9 billion (see Table 6.1 for details).[4] In 1999, the Confederation of Indian Industries reported a total of 216 environmental enterprises operating in India.

According to estimates reported in Table 6.1, the environmental segments requiring the largest investment include wastewater treatment, followed by industrial air pollution. There is also an urgent need for pollution remediation and clean-up services of contaminated surface and ground water that have been polluted through indiscriminate dumping of untreated municipal wastes and wastewater, as well as industrial effluents over the years.

A more recent estimate in 2002 valued the Indian environment market at US$4.36 million, with an annual growth rate of 15%. In 2000, it was estimated at US$3.29 billion and US$3.79 million in 2001. The market estimate included environmental management technology, equipment and services, including clean and renewable energy.[5] Table 6.2 gives the size of the Indian environment market, local production and imports based on the estimates provided by the US Department of Commerce (the US being the single largest exporter of environmental equipment to India). The market has doubled between 1997 and 2002, and while imports are a significant portion of the total market, local production satisfies more than half the market.

Table 6.2 The Environment Market in India (million US $), 1997-2002

Market\Year	1997	1998	1999	2000	2001	2002
Total Market Size	2,170	2,491	2,864	3,294	3,788	4166
Total Local Production	1,302	1,495	1,718	2,061	2,272	2499
Total Imports	868	996	1, 146	1,233	1,516	1667

Source: Compiled from data in *India Country Commercial Guide* 2000, 2002 and FY 2003; Chapter 5 "Leading Sectors for US Exports and Investment". The market estimates include basic water treatment and sanitation projects.

The Indian environment industry consists of two sets of firms: first, large engineering firms offering pollution control equipment or technology packages for pollution treatment along with environmental services; and second, smaller firms specializing in environmental consulting services. In particular, the first type of environmental services has been popular through large turnkey consulting projects involving equipment or technology for pollution treatment, which has been the main focus of the Indian environmental regulation – i.e. the environmental firms typically provide environmental services (related to environmental goods) as part of an integrated package to address an environmental problem, including the provision of engineering, construction, equipment, and operation and maintenance of general utility facilities, such as water, energy, pollution and waste management systems. These Indian firms are typically well developed and large in terms of staff strength and scale of operations (CII 1999).

While the Indian environment industry is nascent, it has made progress in conventional and advanced technologies, both on its own and through joint ventures with foreign manufacturers. The most common pollution abatement products are systems for treating water and controlling air pollution as required by the domestic regulations. The sector has begun to expand to include conservation, resource recovery and waste utilization technologies. The new, as well as upgraded, environmental regulations pertaining to disposal of industrial wastes, municipal solid wastes, noise pollution, etc, at the end of the 1990s, are likely to help in the growth of this sector. For instance, some domestic firms have emerged in refuse treatment and disposal service, especially in composting of municipal solid wastes.

There are also environmental service firms specializing in the provision of environmental study-type services in terms of audit reports, environmental impact assessment (EIA), environmental management system (EMS), auditing, training, etc. Environmental consulting firms from Australia, Denmark, Canada, UK, US, France and Japan have performed EIA studies or pollution prevention studies sponsored by the donor agency of their respective countries. Indian environmental firms have also established affiliations with foreign firms to gain technological know-how/design of pollution abatement equipment (see Table 6.3).

Table 6.3 Selected Foreign Affiliation in the Indian Environment Industry

Indian Company	Foreign Partners
General Electric Company of India Ltd	American Air Filter International SA
Paramount Pollution Control Pvt. Ltd	Anderson
Flakt India	ABB Environmental Services
Hindustan Development Corporation Ltd	C-E Air Preheater Combustion Eng.
Thermax Limited	Babcock & Wilcox, General Electric Environmental Services Inc.
Saraswato Omdistroa; Sumdocate	Smith & Loveless
Humphreys & Glasgow Ltd	Jacobs Engineering Ltd

Source: CII (1996).

The increase in quality certification among Indian firms has promoted the growth of foreign quality assessment and certification services companies in the country: like the American Quality Assessors India Pvt. Ltd and FoodCert-NL, a Netherlands-based quality certification firm in the food and allied processing industry (*Business Line*, July 10, 2001). Registrations in HACCP and hygienic codes of practices of European standards like EN 45011 are certainly on the increase. On the other hand, Indian firms have embraced environmental management systems certification ISO 14001 to signal their environmental consciousness.

Finally, the growth of the environment market in India reflects the increasing environmental spending by Indian industry and the domestic sector. The rise of the Indian packaged water industry (discussed in the previous chapter) reflects the increase in consumer defensive expenditure. Branded bottled drinking water is probably the fastest growing industry in the domestic beverage market. While the market leader is a domestic company (Parle accounting for about 40% of the total market share, with the brand *Bisleri*), multinational firms including Nestle, Danone, Pepsi and Coke have entered the market in a big way buying out small and medium players.[6]

6.3 Environmental Certification of Farms and Firms

As mentioned earlier, the increase in demand for environmental equipment and services in the industrial sector in India during the 1990s stems from three major factors, namely: enhanced domestic environmental regulations and government initiatives; civil society pressure as well as environmental legal activism; and WTO environmental provisions for commodity trade.

Some of the newer domestic environmental regulations in India have particularly encouraged environmental management practices. For instance, mandatory EIA (for 30 categories of activities) and environmental safety audit have boosted the growth of environmental services. Similarly, the Bio-medical Waste Rules (1998), and Hazardous Waste (Management and Handling) Rules (amended 2000) have helped to attract more equipment manufacturers with consulting services in the Indian environment sector.

Indian merchandise exports to developed countries have come under increased pressure for environmental upgradation. Export consignments from developing countries, including India, have been denied market access particularly in OECD markets (rejections at port, as in the case of Indian food consignment refusals in the US discussed in Chapter 4). This has led to a move towards upgrading environmental management systems (like the voluntary ISO 14001, HACCP), as well as obtaining environmental certification and labels in India. The Indian Government too has set up environmental testing and certification laboratories, and helped in environmental training, to enable the exporters to align their products to international environmental demands.

The environmental behavior of Indian firms and farms has thus begun to witness a remarkable change during the post-liberalization era. The analysis here focuses on environmental management behavior, as reflected in the increase in environmental certification and product specific labels, and is divided into two subsections, namely the agricultural and allied sector and the manufacturing sector. While environmental certification by itself does not indicate the improvement in environmental performance of a producing unit, it does reflect the change in the mindset of the Indian businesses to incorporate environmental aspects in their production or processes.

6.3.1 The Agriculture and Allied Export Sector

The certification of food processes and products in the country of origin to ensure quality and safety has increased, especially during the last decade. This has effectively moved costs towards developing countries, since certification often comprises a significant proportion of the total cost of production for exporters in these countries. While the Agreement on SPS (Sanitary and Phytosanitary Measures) is meant to encourage the harmonization of health and safety standards with international standards in food by referring to those set by the Codex Alimentarius Commission (hereafter Codex), its *precautionary principle* (under Article 5.7 even when scientific conclusions are opaque) allows for departures from Codex standards – i.e. countries have the right to set their own standards on say, permissible pesticide residues (if stricter than international norms under the Codex) based on their own risk perception, acceptability and analysis.

In June 2001, the Indian Commerce Ministry noted that non-tariff measures/barriers have affected the Indian exports of fresh fruits, coffee, meat, rice and even herbal medicines. Food safety issues in the developed countries include concerns like BSE (Bovine Spongiform Encephalitis), food poisoning from E-coli and hormone, insecticide and antibiotic residuals in meat, as well as genetically modified organisms in both animal and vegetable products. Indian agricultural exports undergo elaborate testing and certification before being allowed entry into industrialized countries (like the US); beverages have been rejected due to high pesticide residue in Europe/Japan (under the SPS provision of the WTO).

Often individual country health/environmental stipulations are higher than the international benchmark standard. For example, the European Commission's (EC) directive 91/493 requires hygiene standards more stringent than those under the Hazard Analysis Critical Control Point (HACCP)[7] adopted in the Codex. The Indian marine products exporters estimate the compliance cost for meeting the EC norms as 15-40% of free on board value, and while two-thirds of the existing units are estimated to ultimately upgrade to the EC norms, the rest will perish, according to the Indian Marine Products Export Development Agency.

The Indian food processing industry has also been upgrading export-oriented units in response to market access problems in the OECD countries. In the seafood industry, in particular, perhaps the first major jolt for implementation of a quality and risk management system like the HACCP came in 1997 when the EC banned all seafood imports from India. This ban was imposed after the EC team inspected Indian seafood processing units in June 1997.[8] By the end of the same year, in December, the US too made HACCP standards mandatory for seafood processing units (for domestic as well as foreign producers).

The EC ban on Indian seafood in 1997, coupled with import requirements in the US, provided an impetus for the Indian seafood industry to move towards HACCP-based quality control measures in the latter part of the 1990s. Eventually, the EC generated an independent list of approved Indian seafood exporting facilities, which are allowed to export to the EU. Similarly the USFDA maintains a list of 52 Indian seafood units whose consignments of fresh and frozen shrimps bypass the automatic alert system (only subject to random checks). By November 2001, the Export Inspection Council of India approved 113 processing establishments and 8 freezer vessels for export of fish and fishery products to the EU under its mandatory Food Safety Management Systems-based certification scheme.[9]

6.3.1.1 The Move towards Organic Produce and Certification

Diverse limits on chemical tolerance across industrialized countries have segmented the export markets. For example, an ochratoxin limit on the import of coffee enforced in the EU resulted in Indian coffee being rejected by one EU member and then taken at a discount into another, causing loss of foreign exchange and time in the process.[10] For agricultural exports to be marketed as free from chemical residue, organic certification has become important (e.g. that of IFOAM, International Federation of Organic Agriculture Movement).

Though still small at present, the worldwide market for organic food is projected to increase to $102 million by 2010 according to the International Trade Center ($46 million in the EU, $45million in the US and $11million in Japan) from $13 million in 1997. Currently, the US dominates the organic agricultural world trade (being the single largest exporter and importer of organic products). India could experience a boom in this sector if adequately developed. Besides enhanced export earnings, organic farming can help small farmers by reducing financial drain, improving soil fertility, and trimming the government subsidy bill. In the year 2000, the Government of India launched the National Program for Organic Production in view of the optimistic global market expansion. The program targets export expansion in the US and Germany (largest country markets) among others (EXIMIUS, 2001).[11] India's comparative advantage stems from her wealth of indigenous knowledge on organic manure, pesticides, inter-cropping, etc. Moreover, since organic cultivation is labor-intensive, it is especially promising for a populous country like India. As of 1999, only 304 farms were certified to be organic by IFOAM standards, constituting only about 0.001 percent (1,711 hectares) of the total agricultural area in India. In comparison Argentina, Brazil, and China have larger certified tracts under organic cultivation (see Table 6.4).

The export of organic products requires not only farm level certification, but also country level regulation. In particular, the European Commission's mandatory regulation No. 2092/91 on organic products, requires exporting countries to the EU to have standards equivalent to those outlined in the EC regulation. Only six countries are included in the EC list (Article 11-1), while other exporters including those from India are being allowed access via an exception rule (Article 11.6) where the onus of proving equivalence falls on the importer in the EU. This exception rule is valid until 2005.[12] Thus, in 2001, the Indian Government mandated that organic products can be exported, effective from 2001, only if they have been produced, processed and packed under a valid organic certificate (from government accredited agencies, including ENCON, IMO offices in India).

Table 6.4 Certified Organic Farming in Selected Developing Countries, 2000

Country	Year	Organic Farms	Organic Hectares	% of agricultural area
Argentina	2000	1,000	3,000,000	1.770
Brazil	1999	1,200	100,000	0.040
China	2000	-	8,517	0.002
India	**1999**	**304**	**1,711**	**0.001**

Source: Compiled from Tables 7, 13, and 14 in SOL-Survey (2001).

Current organic exports in India include products like organic tea, spices and grains, and there are efforts to increase the organic market in fruits and grains. Peermade Development Society, an NGO in Kerala, the largest Indian exporter of spices, encourages production/export of organic spices from farming communities, especially tribal communities. Among other export houses, Magosan Exports (SKAL certified) has been able to pursue organic farming profitably, and exports spices, honey, coffee, ginger and rice (CSE 20016: 41). Similarly, Indian Organic Food (IFOAM member) profitably trades in organic commodities including rice, tea, grains and sugar cane. Corporate India has decided to put a more concerted effort into promoting organic farming and exports, with a target to get 10,000 farmers across 2000 villages in North India involved in organic farming by 2004, given the global trend in organic food.[13] That indeed would be a welcome step since it would encourage traditional organic farming practices and curb the increasing chemical pollution of land and water.

6.3.2 The Manufactured Export Sector

As environmental trade barriers gained significance in the 1990s, Indian firms found it increasingly essential to signal the eco-sensitivity of their products and production processes. This has been achieved through certification of environmental management systems in production and specific product eco-labels, which have credibility in the target export markets.[14] As observed earlier, traditional Indian exports have faced restrictions in key export markets in Europe and the US. Textile products have been restricted due to the presence of hazardous chemicals like azo-dyes in Europe (e.g. Germany requires certification of azo-dyes free for processed fiber import), inflammability standards in the US, etc. Thus, environmentally upgrading textile units by ISO 14000 standards (ISO 14001 being certifiable) and/or Oko-Tex Standard 1000, signals quality assurance and increases market access in developed country markets for Indian products.

In the last decade, Indian exporters found that importers in developed countries often demand the implementation of environmental management systems as a minimum requirement for business. This has been a powerful driving force for export-oriented firms to move towards standardization and environmental certifications. For example, the large textile firm Century began the phase-out of azo-dyes following the initiation by Otto Aversano, one of the company's major

German clients; another textile firm Arvind Mills Ltd's investment on pollution control equipment was reportedly made to satisfy their customer Marks and Spencer. Similarly Ranbaxy Labs decided to upgrade its manufacturing sites to "zero discharge" sites after queries on environmental standards from its customer Hoechst.

Importer induced production process upgradation has also been observed in the leather industry. For instance, use of a toxic chemical was phased out in leather processing units in India after the fungicide pentachlorophenol (PCP) was banned in Europe (beginning with Germany in 1989) and the US. Here too, the industry structure (small-scale export units) was the major problem, and the small units survived with support from government and/or importer initiatives. Indian leather tanneries had to switch to substitutes like Busan 30, which costs ten times more than PCP (Jha 1997: 121). The PCP substitutes had to be imported from Germany or the US and the Indian government facilitated the import of other substitutes (such as chemicals like TCMTB and PCMC) by reducing import duties. The Indo-German Export Promotion Project helped in information dissemination and testing facilities for leather tanneries.

The example of the leather industry illustrates a more general problem faced by a developing country like India, which starts using and manufacturing certain chemicals after a lag period from the industrialized countries. It reflects the lag in technology flow across industrialized and industrializing countries: by the time developing countries set up the manufacture of the chemicals, they may have been banned or restricted abroad.

6.3.2.1 The Case of Environmental Certification among Indian Firms

The ISO 14001 certification is one of the most popular tools to indicate environment friendly management systems worldwide. In an effort to signal credible environmental management systems, the number of ISO 14001 certifications by Indian firms have increased significantly over the last six years, after this environmental management system became certifiable. Table 6.5 shows the total ISO 14001 certified units in India, compared to those in China and Thailand. In India, since the base in quality certification with ISO 9000 has been quite extensive, it has helped to move towards certification in an environmental management system. Since most ISO 14001 certified Indian firms are also ISO 9000 certified, data on both are reported, since the latter represents the potential pool for environmental management certifications.

While the increase in ISO 14001 certifications registered a remarkable growth over the years, the response of Indian companies has been slow compared to companies in other Asian developing countries like China and Thailand. The number of ISO 14001 certifications in India increased from 1 in 1995 to 28 in 1997, and further to 400 in 2001 (see Table 6.5). While India seemed ahead with one certified firm compared to none in the other two countries in 1995, over the years certifications in China and Thailand outstripped India. In fact, China registered one of the highest growth rates worldwide in ISO environmental certifications!

Table 6.5 ISO 14001 and 9000 Certifications in India, 1995-2001

Country		1995	1996	1997	1998	1999	2000	2001
India	14001	1	2	28	40	111	257	400
	9000	1023	1665	2865	3344	5200	5682	5554
China	14001	-	9	22	94	222	510	1085
	9000	507	3406	5698	8245	15109	25657	57783
Thailand	14001	-	58	61	126	229	310	483
	9000	143	182	1104	1236	1527	2553	3870

Note: the figures correspond to certifications until December of each year.

Source: The ISO Survey - Eleventh Cycle, 2002.

Environmental certifications are costly, and thus typically larger plants find it easier to absorb the cost. Indeed, a cross-country survey of ISO 14001-certified Indian firms (Nyati 2000), found that of the seventy-one firms covered, most units were large in size. Twenty-five units were under the category of small and medium enterprises (SMEs) but almost all turned out to be medium sized. Yet, small-scale production units characterize some of the key export industries in India, for example the textile industry, where the share of SMEs in Indian exports is about 80% (WTO 1996). However, the promise of market expansion in the textile sector, especially with the phase-out of quotas under the MFA (Multi Fiber Agreement under the new WTO Agreement on Textiles and Clothing by the year 2004), makes it imperative for Indian firms to undertake environmental upgradation even in smaller production units.

Businesses view environmental certification as a new competitive tool in product differentiation in the global market. The survey of ISO 14001-certified firms in India suggests that the predominant reason for certification is indeed the corporate image, and the decision to implement the environmental management system and obtain certification seemed related to the size of the domestic market and exports (Nyati 2000). In the transport sector, the leading car manufacturer in India, Maruti Udyog Ltd (a joint venture company until the year 2002, and now converted to 100% foreign ownership) became the first passenger car manufacturing company in India to acquire ISO 14001 certification (at its Gurgaon plant) in December 1999. The company observed that one of the main reasons for adopting the environmental management system was to build a green corporate image and facilitate better access to international and domestic markets.

Firm characteristics like type of ownership, parentage, and number of locations, do not appear to be related to the decision to implement the environmental management system (Nyati 2000). This corroborates the independent survey of MNC subsidiaries in India, which observed that environmental management certification was not prevalent among the survey units (Ruud 2002).

Among the benefits of ISO 14001 certification, Indian firms have reported reduced costs, increased competitiveness and international market opportunities. For example, a medium sized garment exporting firm Prem Group in Tirupur, state of Tamil Nadu, reported cost savings of about $100,000 (over Rs 45 lakhs) per annum from ISO 14001 programs which reduced consumption of water, energy, dyes, etc (Prakash 2001). Increase in both productivity and quality of manufacturing is reported as a combined effect of ISO 14000 and SA 8000 program implementation in the firm.

Besides ISO environmental certification, there are other instances of product level certification and environmental up-gradation induced by importer pressure. Specific product eco-labels have become important to gain market access (or market expansion) in OECD countries. The first Indian firm to obtain the German Oko-Tex certification was Century Textiles (with the largest textile mill in Asia) in 1995. The company's marketing department felt that it could get a 10-15% better rate than before due to the eco-label. The company reported that the market widened by at least 15% in the first year, and new buyers from the US and UK had come in. Another textile firm, Arvind Mills of India, the second largest denim producer in the world, undertook expensive pollution-abatement investment to acquire the Oko-Tex label to promote its exports. It commissioned a plant for Rs 120 crores (about US$ 30 million) in 1998, to qualify as a zero discharge firm with an eye on the prospects for exports to developed countries.[15]

Notes

[1]   Maturity in an industry is characterized by decelerating growth, heightened competition, reduced profitability, growing customer sophistication, pricing pressure, emphasis on marketing (by firms), consolidation of market share by larger players, and heightened merger and acquisition activities.

[2]   Based on Census 1991 and 2001 figures, the total population increased from 846 million in 1991 to 1,027 million in 2001, while the urban population increased from 215.7 million to 285.3 million during the same period. Urban population has been increasing due to natural population increase, reclassification of new towns and rural-urban migration.

[3]   While the US Department of Commerce estimates the current size of the environment market in India to be $4 billion, growing at an annual rate of 15%, an Indo-German Chamber of Commerce estimated the market to be almost double the size at $8 billion. Of the 14 sectors identified as best prospects for investment in India in the year 2002 on the basis of Indian imports from the US, the sector of pollution control equipment ranked sixth. The major areas of investment included: water, wastewater treatment, recycling and sanitation; industrial and vehicular air pollution control; hazardous waste management, treatment and disposal; biomedical waste management; municipal solid waste management; pollution testing and monitoring equipment/services; clean and renewable energy equipment; and environmental consulting/engineering services.

[4]   CII (1996). Note, however, that the estimate was conservative since it did not cover segments like industrial non-hazardous solid waste treatment or sanitation. The estimates were based on secondary data collected from government agencies, industry suppliers and multilateral and bilateral assistance agencies.

[5]   *US Country Commercial Guide for India* 2002, 2003.

[6]   Bhushan (2002).

[7]   The HACCP system was enforced by the US in 1997 and subsequently followed by several countries on imports of seafood. Today it has become a major barrier to India's seafood exports in the industrialized countries.

[8] Menon, P. and R. Ramachandran (1997) "Contamination Scare: Indian Seafood Exports". However, it is true that the causes of contamination can be traced to the fishing harbor, fishing boats and landing centers, and not just the peeling sheds.

[9] However, there are 199 EIC fish processing certified units for exports to other countries, where standards are less stringent than those in the EU (DOC *Annual Report 2001-02*).

[10] "NTBs scuttling farm exports: report", page 18, *The Economic Times*, Bangalore, 28 June 2001.

[11] This is rather belated, compared to the Chinese efforts. The China Green Food Development Center, under the Ministry of Agriculture, was set up in 1992 to certify agricultural produce.

[12] EC (2000): 21.

[13] PTI news, December 7th, 2001, Press Trust of India.

[14] Developing countries have also come up with eco-labels, like India's eco-mark. However, eco-labels prevalent in developed countries have more credibility for developed country markets.

[15] Mr Nyati, Confederation of Indian Industries, New Delhi, 1999.

Chapter 7

Public Participation in Pollution Management

7.1 Pollution Control Regime in India

India being a large diverse country, the nature of environmental problems and challenges varies across geographical regions, states and communities. The stakeholders in environmental management are broadly the government regulators, the industry and the community. The previous chapters elaborated the changes that have been taking place through new environmental regulations, industrial and consumption behavior, as well as the emergence of the new environment industry in India following greater global integration. Besides these factors, the civil society of the country has played an important role in the present evolving pollution management regime. This chapter analyzes the role of civil society, the third stakeholder, in pollution management through the legal system.

Environmental management policies can be broadly analyzed under first, pollution and waste management strategies; and second, natural resource management strategies. In Indian cities, where pollution has reached alarming levels causing adverse health problems, attention has been focused on mitigating emissions (particularly that of atmospheric pollutants). In the villages, where the rural livelihood largely depends on the productivity of the natural resource base, the conservation efforts have been largely in terms of forests and watershed management. While government regulations over the years have covered substantial ground in terms of sectors to address both natural resource and pollution management, there have been major deficiencies in terms of monitoring and enforcement of these regulations. The civil society has supplemented for the deficiencies in government regulation and monitoring of pollution in India. This chapter focuses in particular on public participation in pollution management.

When government policies or market behavior fail to correct the environmental distortions in the economy (in neoclassical framework, when market prices of goods and services do not reflect their "true" prices), the community can induce both the government and the industry to take action and correct the adverse effects in the system. In other words, the community can potentially play a significant role in the environmental pollution management of an economy besides the government (regulator) and the industry. In environmentally conscious societies, governments adopt stricter environmental policies when political support is determined by the environmental sensitivity of its policies (based on the voting communities' priorities), and thereby drive the market to incorporate the true environmental costs of the system. Not surprisingly, community participation in environmental management has been recognized across the globe as an important element in the process of sustainable economic development.

In theory, the optimal level of environmental quality can be achieved through different regimes, and three such regimes are popularly considered in the literature. First, following Coase (1960), property rights of environmental resources can be defined and the economic agents can decide on the desired level of pollution (given their true costs and benefits from pollution) through mutual negotiations. Since according to the Coase theorem, as long as property rights are well defined and transaction costs are negligible, the polluting agents and victims of pollution can arrive at the optimal equilibrium through negotiations (provided the total number of players is small).[1] Second, under a command and control (CAC) approach, the regulator can enforce the environmental standards based on the optimal level of pollution (where the social marginal cost equals social marginal benefit of pollution). As long as these standards are enforced, the social optimum can be achieved. Third, the regulator can adopt economic or market-based instruments (MBIs) to abate pollution, and these cover instruments that harness self-interest of economic agents for environmental goals. MBIs include price-related instruments like pollution taxes and permits, as well as indirect economic instruments like the law of liability for damages and environmental information disclosure systems (Paulus 1995). The use of these economic instruments triggers the industry into innovating with cheaper ways to cut down on pollution and encourages firm action that projects a more environmentally friendly image in the market (through the information disclosure system). On the whole, MBIs are expected to achieve the optimum at the least cost to the economy (compared to uniform CAC standards).

In most countries across the globe, CAC measures including standards on emissions and effluents from different polluting sources – whether stationary point sources like firms or mobile point sources like vehicles – define the pollution abatement regime. In developed countries, the CAC regime is largely complemented with economic instruments: for example, the US has by far the most extensive use of tradable pollution permits in the world, and in Europe pollution taxes are more in vogue. Even developing countries have utilized economic incentives to induce pollution reduction in industry. A Coasian type of bargaining to control industrial pollution has been documented in Asian countries, including Japan and Indonesia, between local inhabitants and plant management (O'Connor 1995, Pargal and Wheeler 1995, Hettige et al 1996). According to a World Bank study in India, however, community pressures (in terms of proxy measures of better-educated and higher income communities) do not seem to induce lower pollution (Pargal, et al 1997), but communities do seem to have a significant effect on the level of inspections.[2]

This chapter contends that community pressure in India has played a significant role, quite distinct from those documented in the other Asian countries, through the environmental public interest litigation (PIL). The civil society (individuals and environmental NGOs) in India has been active in bringing polluters to court with environmental public interest litigation, since a good environment is a constitutional right of the Indian citizen (under the *Right to Life*). Some of the Supreme Court rulings from the environmental public interest litigation have resulted in major regulatory initiatives (leading to the development of new and stricter environmental legislations), and have also influenced firm behaviour. The establishment of the law of liability of environmental damages (polluter pays principle) endorsed by these cases has led to indirect market pressure on polluting agents in India especially during the 1990s. This in turn has been one of the factors that has helped in the growth of the environment market (both equipment and services) in the country.

7.2 Deficiencies in the Current Regime and Environmental PIL

In India, the pollution control regime is almost purely of the CAC nature, supplemented by economic incentives and some environmental management procedures, as discussed earlier in chapter 3. The environmental quality standards have been defined by sector (e.g. industrial pollution norms spell out effluent standards by source), as well as by location (e.g. air/noise quality norms by residential, industrial and sensitive areas). The economic instruments used in pollution management in India include: subsidies on catalytic converters/ compressed natural gas for vehicles; benefits for industrial pollution control equipment; and fines and/or imprisonment for violation of environmental norms.

The Indian domestic environmental legislation can be considered to be fairly well developed, yet despite the existence of elaborate pollution standards, the problem in controlling pollution arises from the poor enforcing of the standards. Attention has been focused on *initial* compliance (installation of abatement equipment) rather than *continuous* compliance of actual effluent concentration (and ensuring the installed equipment is actually operating). In effect, pollution would not reduce after installation because pollution equipment is not running, i.e. the pollution load in the system can keep increasing even if all polluters were to comply with the regulations.[3] Indeed Pargal et al (1997) found that plant-level pollution is unaffected by formal inspections by State Pollution Control Boards (SPCBs) in India, since firms probably activate the equipment only when inspections are scheduled.

Also ambient and source standards are set independently, unrelated in terms of the volume of pollution generation; thus it is possible for environmental quality to deteriorate despite a high degree of compliance among individual polluters. The fines and penalties for non-compliance are low in India, and the penalty structure is insensitive to the degree of default, since the same penalty is charged for violation of environmental standards irrespective of the size of violation (whether small or large) or the pattern of offense (occasional or repeated violations).

The problem in achieving the optimum (assuming the standards indeed reflect the optimum equilibrium) arises from the difficulty of enforcing these environmental standards.[4] The effective monitoring by the SPCBs is poor and the lack of comprehensive data/information on polluting activities of industries exacerbates the problem (since by law, the SPCB has the entire burden of proof of any offense by an industrial unit). The SPCBs often tolerate non-complying units due to the work overload at the boards, lack of staff, budget, equipment and facilities. About 65% of the members in seventeen state PCBs were found to be technically incompetent to do a job that required high technical skill (*Down to Earth*, July 31, 2001). Since the boards are expected to generate funds through consent fees, and other charges, lack of proper monitoring and implementation in turn translates into inadequate fund generation. Even when cases are filed by the PCBs against erring firms, they remain pending for years in the lower courts.

The merits of using economic instruments like industrial pollution taxes were recognized in the 1992 Policy Statement on Pollution Abatement of the Ministry of Environment and Forests, and the implementation of market-based instruments in India are in the pipeline.[5] The government also issued the National Conservation Strategy and Policy Statement on Environment and Development in 1992 that recognized the role of non-government organizations (NGOs), industries and the public to preserve resources and protect the environment while ensuring developmental activities. Indeed, during the last 15 years, the inadequacy in the enforcement of environmental norms and the rapid rise in pollution levels have prompted public interest environmental litigation and the rise of judicial activism in India's environmental management.

Coupled with the increase in environmental PIL, the role of the Indian community in pollution control regimes has increased through public hearings in environmental impact assessment procedures for economic activities. Since 1997, development activities including industrial projects, thermal power plants, mining projects, river valley hydro-electric schemes, infrastructure projects, etc (30 categories in total) have mandatory public hearings in order to completely assess the environmental impact before being granted clearance by the state. However, the small-scale industries were exempt from a public hearing in a draft notification in 2001. The current trend of active participation of Indian citizens in pollution control management will continue to grow. Moreover, this trend perfectly matches with the 1992 National Environmental Strategy and Policy Statement, which recognized the important role of the public and NGOs in protecting the environment during the process of economic development.

The environmental PIL and the accompanying judicial activism experienced in India are both reactionary as well as progressive.[6] Although judicial activism has had limited impact, it certainly has succeeded in becoming a significant factor in the rubric of the country's pollution management system. While formal enforcement remains weak in India, the constitutional right of the polluted agents has become an important instrument of pollution control.

Since judicial activism has been most significant through the Supreme Court (SC) rulings, this chapter considers some of the most significant SC case rulings impacting environmental management in two polluting sectors. The SC has given rulings in a wide range of environmental issues including industrial pollution, vehicular pollution, protection and conservation of forests, urban and solid waste management, protection and conservation of wild life, etc.[7] Of these sectors, the analysis here concentrates on the two polluting sectors – namely the industrial and the transport sector from which pollution loads have been increasing. The next section briefly discusses the major pollution problems in Indian cities, and analyzes why the industrial and transport sectors have been under the scrutiny of the public and the judiciary.

7.3 Target Pollution Sectors in Indian Cities: Industry and Transport

Urbanization in India has brought with it the air and water pollution problems similar to that experienced in most cities around the world. Indeed, as noted earlier, during the early 1990s, the capital city of Delhi was judged to be the fourth most polluted city in the world! Although economic growth in urban India has been higher than the national average, the quality of life in the cities is deteriorating due to increasing pollution. Pollution management efforts in recent years have significantly targeted the transport and industrial sectors, and largely ignored the household sector. It is noteworthy that some of the policies have resulted from public interest litigations, and this section analyzes the implications of this form of people's participation in India's pollution management.

Along with economic development, Indian cities have witnessed phenomenal deterioration of quality in ambient air, water, land and noise. In many cities, industrial and residential areas overlap due to unplanned (sometimes unauthorized) development and construction. Today more than 300 million Indians live in the cities, thus damage from urban pollution affects a large population base. About 35 Indian cities carry a population of more than 1 million people, and more than 20% of the city population lives in slums, and faces high health risks from poor environmental quality. The health costs of pollution are largely borne by the urban poor, since their slums are often close to open drains with untreated sewage, household garbage, and also chemical pollutants from factories.

As in other metropolitan cities across the globe, air pollution problems have been judged to be the most severe pollution problem in urban India. A study of air quality data for suspended particulate matter in 70 Indian cities in 1997 revealed that only 19 cities had pollutant levels below the permissible limit![8] The degradation of urban air quality has stemmed mostly from the road transport sector. The number of vehicles on city roads has increased phenomenally and vehicular emissions have been identified as the most important source of outdoor air pollution in Indian megacities, (followed by domestic and industrial emissions).

On the other hand, the degradation of fresh water is largely caused by the domestic sector (followed by industrial effluents and agricultural run-off). Domestic wastewater constitutes 64% of total wastewater by volume (domestic and industrial) generated in urban centres, and sewage treatment facilities are grossly inadequate (MOEF 2003: Chapter 5). City sewage is the main source of river pollution in India, followed by industrial effluents. Water quality monitoring records suggest that organic and bacterial contamination is the most critical problem of surface water (as indicated by an increase in biological oxygen demand, BOD values) during 1990-99.[9] Even though 74% of the municipal wastewater generated is collected, only 24% undergoes some form of treatment before disposal.[10] Numerous illegal urban industrial units continue to discharge untreated effluents into the drains, rivers and land, due to lack of adequate monitoring. While it is true that pollution legislation is openly violated, in some cases legislation is incomplete: for example, while the Water Act covers industrial effluent standards, it ignores domestic and municipal effluents even though they constitute 90% of India's wastewater volume!

Of course, land pollution (as also ground water pollution) from solid waste generation has also increased in the cities. At present per capita waste generation in an Indian city ranges from 0.2-0.6 kgs per day, with collection efficiency between 50-90% across the cities (CPCB 1999b, 1999c). The composition of solid wastes has also undergone a change with the change in consumption pattern in the cities. The focus of community participation through environmental PIL in pollution management in India has been by far the greatest in the industrial and transport sectors.

7.3.1 The Case of Air Pollution: Major Pollutants and Emission Sources

The Central Pollution Control Board of India has recognized that suspended particulate matter (SPM) is one of the major atmospheric pollutants in urban India during 1990-99 (CPCB 2001: 44). In fact the maximum number of violations of air quality standards in the country have been for SPM. The pollution from SPM includes both non-respirable and respirable fine/ultra fine particulate matter, and poses a severe threat to the health of the citizens. The problem is especially acute in the residential areas of most major cities, where SPM standards are routinely violated. The major sources of SPM include vehicular emissions, frequent use of private power generators, and extensive use of fossil fuels and biomass.

Table 7.1 shows the number of monitoring stations (in cities) that violated annual standards by more than 2% in the year 1999 by individual criteria pollutants, to illustrate that the problem of high SPM in residential areas seems the most critical in Indian cities.

While SPM non-attainment is dispersed throughout the country, the problem is most severe in the North-West part of the country. In South India, the problem is not as grave probably due to a more dense vegetation cover, mountainous terrain and ventilation effects due to the sea breeze and land breeze.

Considering the five most populous cities in India today – Mumbai, Delhi, Kolkata, Bangalore and Chennai – the levels of SPM in residential areas during 1990-98 have been at dangerously high levels, and in violation of Indian standards, except for Chennai (see Table 7A.2 in the appendix). In particular, increased levels of SPM have led to a steep rise in respiratory problems in the young. A study of health costs of SPM pollution (considering non-trauma deaths) in Delhi concluded that more life years can be saved in the city for a given SPM reduction than in the US, because the largest impact occurs in the 15-44 age group in India.[11]

Table 7.1 Violations of Annual Atmospheric Standards in Stations, 1999

Area Class	SO$_2$	NO$_2$	SPM
Residential	1	3	37
Industrial	2	0	8
Sensitive	0	1	2
Total	*3*	*4*	*47*

Note: Of the total 139 monitoring stations in the cities/towns with adequate data for assessment, 68 were in residential, 68 in industrial and 3 in sensitive areas.

Source: CPCB 2001: 44.

While urban air quality management in India has focused on the monitoring of particulate matter and sulfur/nitrogen oxides, other pollutants like carbon monoxide, lead, benzene, ozone, and poly-aromatic hydrocarbons have been only sporadically monitored, or only in selected cities like Delhi, if at all! Air quality monitoring was initiated in India in 1984-85 under the National Air Quality Monitoring program, which now has 290 monitoring stations covering 90 cities across the country (operated under the network of various pollution control boards and research institutions). Air quality standards in India are differentiated by residential, industrial and sensitive areas, and the air quality data is also classified accordingly (see Table 7A.1 at the end of the chapter for details).

The relative contribution of different sectors to air pollution is well illustrated by considering the case of Delhi, one of the fastest growing cities in India. Vehicles are by far the most important source of air pollution in the city followed by the industrial sector and the domestic sector (see Table 7.2). While the human population in Delhi increased fourfold during 1961-93, motor vehicle registration in the city increased by more than 51 times. The total number of vehicles in the city outnumbers those in the cities of Mumbai, Kolkata or Chennai, even though the former two are more populous than Delhi. In the 1970s, the industrial sector accounted for the major pollution load in the atmosphere, but by the mid-1990s the growth in the vehicle population made the transport sector the largest emission source. (Table 7A.3 at the end of the chapter gives the vehicular emission pollution load in the five most populous Indian cities in 1996.) Thus, much of the public interest litigation on the environment have addressed the transport and industrial sectors – the two main sources of atmospheric pollution, as discussed in the next section.

Table 7.2 Sector Contribution to Atmospheric Pollution in Delhi, 1970-2001

Source\ Year	1970-71	1980-81	1990-91	2000-01
Industrial	56	40	29	20
Vehicular	23	42	63	72
Domestic	21	18	8	8

Figures indicate percentage share.

Note: Industrial sector includes thermal power plants.

Source: CPCB (2000a).

It is important to note that although outdoor air pollution has been covered here, another severe problem is that of indoor air pollution, especially among the poorer households. The problem is pervasive among both urban as well as rural poor households, since they rely mostly on traditional biomass energy like fuel-wood, agricultural wastes, crop and animal residue, which lead to toxic fumes. Traditional biomass fuel sources constitute 40% of total energy consumption in India (MOEF 2001), and provides 80% of the rural energy for cooking. Biomass smoke in homes is estimated to cause half a million premature deaths each year, mostly of women and children, who are exposed to high concentrations of toxic pollutants. Indoor air pollution problems are being tackled through better design of cooking stoves, ventilation of kitchens and also educating women about the health hazards from exposure to these kitchen fumes.

7.4 Environmental Property Rights: Advantage Indian Citizens

The degradation of living conditions has prompted Indian society to seek remedy through civil action. A good environment is a constitutional right of all Indian citizens under the *Right to Life* (Article 21), and the protection of the environment is a fundamental duty of each citizen (Article 51A). These provisions have been used especially by the Supreme Court in dealing with environmental cases, and considering environmental, ecological, air, water pollution, etc. as amounting to violation of Article 21. This interpretation of the fundamental right to life entitles citizens to invoke the writ jurisdiction of the Supreme Court and the High Courts. There has been a clear movement towards public interest litigations to reduce pollution in India, some of which have had far-reaching consequences. This seemingly pseudo-Coasian approach in India has brought industries and industrial estates to court in lieu of the negotiating table between polluters and victims of the Coase model, implemented with reasonable success in Indonesia (O'Connor 1995, World Bank 2000).

Apart from the Indian Constitution, the environmental legislation also has provisions for polluter prosecution. Under section 16 of the Environment Protection Act 1986 (EPA), a company, if deemed a polluter, is punishable for that offense. The "cognizance of offense" clause of the EPA (section 19), the Air Act (amended 1987) and the Water Act (amended 1988) allows any citizen to prosecute a polluting firm provided a notice of at least 60 days is given to the polluter. Citizens have a right to information on polluters from pollution control boards for the purpose of prosecution (section 43 of the Air Act, amended 1987, and section 49 of the Water Act, amended 1988). For granting compensation for environmental damages, the courts have used provision under the Public Liability Insurance Act (1991) and the Factories Act (1995).[12]

Several of the public litigation cases have resulted in polluting units been closed down or relocated away from residential areas, and more importantly ushered in new regulations (in the road transport sector) during the last decade. In some cases, the principle of polluter pays has been evoked and damages to restore the environment imposed on polluting units. In a recent ruling in March 2002, the Supreme Court clarified:

> Pollution as a civil wrong… a Tort committed against the community as a whole. A person, therefore guilty of causing pollution has to pay damages (compensation) for restoration of the environment and ecology. He has also to pay damages to those who have suffered loss on account of the act of the offender. The powers of this Court under Article 32 are not restricted and it can award damages in a PIL or a Writ Petition as has been held in series of decisions. In addition to damages aforesaid, the person guilty of causing pollution can also be held liable to pay exemplary damages so that it may act as a deterrent for others not to cause pollution in any manner.
>
> *(Ruling dated March 15, 2002, in Beas River Case of Mehta v. Kamal Nath*
> *WP182/1996)*

The increase in environmental PIL and judicial activism (prompted by individuals as well as by NGOs) during the past 15 years, began to be perceived as a significant threat by polluting units across the country.

The establishment of the law of liability has created a deterrent effect on pollution by creating an incentive for polluters to limit the risk of environmental damages. Thus while formal enforcement remains weak in India, the constitutional right of the victims of pollution has become an important instrument of pollution control. In particular, civil action has helped focus the regulator's attention on important pollution sectors like road transport (which is a major source of urban air pollution as seen in the previous section) and industries (some of which have been releasing toxic pollutants directly into the waterways or land), and has ushered in new environmental regulations.

7.4.1 Public Interest Litigation for Vehicular Pollution Control

Prior to 1990, India had no environmental standards for vehicles. The new rules for cleaner vehicles on city roads largely followed from Supreme Court rulings in public interest litigations to reduce urban air pollution. The first petition was filed in 1985 by Supreme Court Advocate M. C. Mehta (*M.C. Mehta v. Union of India* WP 13029/1985), and a spurt of rulings followed in the 1990s. In 1990-91, the pollution generated by vehicles increased substantially and the Supreme Court recognized the need for action.

Table 7.3 lists some of the major SC rulings on vehicular pollution. Some of the most significant rulings of the Supreme Court for vehicular pollution cases during 1990 through 2001 resulted in mandatory measures to reduce pollution from city road transport.

During the mid-1990s leaded petrol was phased out, first in the five metrocities of Delhi, Mumbai, Kolkata, Chennai and Bangalore, and then in the rest of India. In 1999, the older commercial fleet was also phased out in Delhi, and in 2001 a conversion to single fuel mode of natural compressed gas was ordered in the city. While the latter measures have been implemented in Delhi, which gained the notoriety of being the most polluted Indian city in the early 1990s (and the fourth most polluted city in the world), these measures are bound to spread to other cities in the country.

Thus in effect, environmental standards for vehicles were introduced in India in 1990, and the subsequent notifications made them more stringent in 1992, 1996 and 2000. Euro-I norms were implemented in 2000 throughout the country for all categories of vehicles. Bharat Stage-II norms, comparable to Euro-II, for vehicles (see Table 7A.4 in appendix for details) were implemented in a phased manner starting with the National Capital Region (including Delhi) in 2000, and extended to other cities like Mumbai, Kolkata and Chennai in 2001.

Table 7.3 Major Supreme Court Rulings on Vehicular Pollution, 1990-2002

Case (year of ruling)	Court Ruling
1. Seriousness of issues (1990)	Rise in vehicle (petrol & diesel) main cause of pollution. Registration of defective vehicles to be suspended, effective 1991.
2. Need for strategic action (1991)	Delhi Transport Corporation identified as one of the most notorious polluters in the city (plying thousands of polluting buses). Campaign to increase pollution awareness among all automobile owners. Committee on vehicular pollution in Delhi to be constituted by 1991.
3. Lead phase out of all vehicles (1994)	Lead-free petrol to be sold in all outlets of the four cities of Delhi, Mumbai, Kolkata and Chennai, and catalytic converters for petrol-driven cars made available by April 1995. Order to supply low-lead petrol (maximum lead content of 0.15g/l) in the entire country by December 1996.
4. Government vehicles (1996)	All official government cars are to be fitted with catalytic converters or a CNG kit by August 1996.
5. Ban on old commercial/ transport vehicles (1998)	All commercial and transport vehicles more than 15 years old (totaling 15,511) not permitted to ply in the national capital region of Delhi after December 1998.
6. Buses to use natural gas (2001)	Commercial vehicles in Delhi should convert to single fuel mode of CNG, effective April 2001.
7. Phasing out of diesel buses (2002)	Diesel buses in Delhi to be phased out at a rate of 800 diesel buses per month starting from May 1, 2002, till all the diesel buses are replaced. Fine of Rs. 500/- per bus per day imposed on diesel bus owners operating beyond January 31, 2002. Fine to increase to Rs. 1,000/day after 30 days of operation of the diesel buses with effect from May 6, 2002. Director of Delhi Transport to collect the fine and deposit at the SC by the tenth day of every month.

Source: Compiled from legal cases listed in Legal and Scientific Resources for Asia.

Another noteworthy aspect of the Supreme Court rulings on vehicular pollution is that the health costs of vehicular exhaust have been explicitly recognized. In a recent ruling in May 2002 on vehicular pollution, the SC noted that the adverse health effect statistics, especially the sharp rise in instances of respiratory diseases among children, indicate that the effect of "continuing air pollution" is more "devastating than what was caused by the Bhopal gas tragedy". The ruling quoted research, which has indicated that cancer potency of diesel vehicles is more than two times that of petrol vehicles in India. For example, the carcinogenic effect of particulate matter from one new diesel car is equivalent to 24 petrol cars and 84 new CNG cars on the road.[13] The SC ruled that diesel buses in Delhi be completely phased out, at a rate of 800 diesel buses/ month beginning May 1, 2002.

7.4.2 Public Interest Litigation and Industrial Pollution Control

As in other countries, the community in India has also served as informal regulator, given that monitoring (and hence probability of formal detection of pollution violation) is low. In particular, in India, public interest environmental litigation has served as a proxy for formal implementation of pollution regulation during the last fifteen years (beginning in the mid-1980s), since enforcement of the CAC environmental measures have been poor. Although the SPCBs have the authority to cut off water and electricity or close down non-compliant plants, they have been averse to resort to such measures on the defaulters for a variety of reasons.[14]

Moreover, since only medium- and large-scale industrial units are included in the regulation purview of the pollution control boards, the small-scale industries (SSIs), which are significant polluters (but difficult to monitor) are not monitored by the authorities. The SSI sector comprises a vast number of very small enterprises, many of which are in the informal sector and may not even be registered.[15] According to one estimate, SSIs in India (more than 3 million) contribute to 65% of the total industrial pollution load, and to 40% of industrial production (*Down to Earth July 31, 2001*). Environmental PILs have also targeted the illegal location of SSIs in urban residential areas.

Not surprisingly, surrogate environmental enforcement through judicial activism became especially prevalent following public interest litigations. The high courts (at the state level, e.g. in the cities of Delhi, Chennai, Mumbai) as well as the Supreme Court have made significant rulings. The filing of public interest environmental litigations began systematically in the mid-1980s, while the spurt of court rulings was observed in the 1990s. The cases have covered effluent pollution from industries into air, water and land.

The rulings in the SC resulted from the writ petitions filed by the noted Supreme Court advocate, M.C. Mehta, as well as NGOs. Table 7.4 highlights eleven such Supreme Court rulings in urban industrial pollution cases.

The Delhi land use cases resulted from the original petition in 1985 (*Mehta v. Union of India* WP4677/1985). The Bichhri industrial case ruling was in response to a writ petition filed by an NGO (ICELA original writ petition WP967/1989, plus other petitions WP94/1990, 824/1993 and 76/1994). Similarly the Tamil Nadu tanneries case was filed by an NGO, Vellore Citizens' Welfare Forum (WP914/1991). The Kolkata tanneries ruling in 1996 is part of a set of rulings against leather tanneries resulting from an original writ petition filed in 1985 (*Mehta v. Union of India* WP 3727/1985) under which tanneries in Kanpur were also closed down in the 1980s.

It is important to note here that in dealing with the PILs on industrial pollution, the Supreme Court made it clear that:

> ...the petitions alleging environmental pollution caused by private industrial units were not as much against those private units as against the Union of India, the state government, and the pollution control boards ... which were supposed to prevent environmental hazards. Their failure to perform their statutory duties resulted in the violation of the right of the residents to life and liberty guaranteed by article 21 of the Constitution.
>
> *(Sathe, 2002: 224).*

Table 7.4 Selected Supreme Court Rulings on Polluting Industries, 1992-2002

Case (ruling year)	Court Ruling
1. Delhi stone crushers (June 1992)	Mechanical stone crushers in the union territory of Delhi to be closed, effective August 15, 1992.
2. Bichhri industrial pollution (February 1996)	Sealing of chemical factories in Bichhri. Ministry of Environment and Forests asked to determine damage costs of toxic sludge in soil and water, and recover the cost from the industries to restore the environment. A fine of Rs 50,000 on the industry to pay petitioner ICELA, to encourage other voluntary bodies to bring in public interest litigation.
3. Coastal Zone Case (April 1996)	Pollution caused by industries in coastal regions (of Maharashtra and Goa) to be dealt with by respective high courts. Central government was asked to set up state Coastal Management Authorities and also a National Coastal Management Authority.
4. Delhi hazardous industries (July 1996)	168 industries asked to relocate from Delhi to any other industrial estate in the NCR, and stop functioning in Delhi, effective November 30, 1996. Employees in these industrial units to be compensated for the disruption.
5. Tamil Nadu tanneries case (August 1996)	Central government asked to constitute an authority to estimate the damage cost of pollution based on the Precautionary Principle and the Polluter Pays Principle. Tanneries (about 700) not paying these damages are to be closed down. Rs 10,000 fine each on the tanneries to be paid by October 31, 1996. Fine and damage revenue to constitute an Environment Protection Fund, and used for compensating people and rectifying the environment. Effluent treatment plants to be set up by November 30, 1996.
6. Delhi illegal industries (October 1996)	39,000 illegal industrial units operating in residential areas of Delhi ordered to close down.
7. Badkhal Lake and Surajkund (October 1996)	No construction to be allowed within the green belt of Badkhal Lake and Surajkund, except a small area for recreational and tourism purposes.
8. Delhi hazardous industries (December 1996)	Industries could not relocate unless they protected the workers and pay according to compensation terms of the Industrial Dispute Act (1947) to workers who refuse to relocate, plus one year's wages. Industries closing down have to pay workers six years' wages.
9. Tanneries case: Kolkata (December 1996)	Tanneries in eastern Kolkata ordered to close down and relocate to a new complex by September 1997. Pollution fine of Rs 10,000 imposed on each tannery (total about 550) to be paid by February 1997, for damages to the environment (under an Environment Protection Fund). Workers unable to relocate to be paid six years wages as compensation.
10. Delhi brick kilns (August 2000)	Brick kilns in agricultural land have to change over to fly ash technology or close down.
11. Beas River (March 2002)	Damage cost based on Polluter Pays Principle of Rs 10 lakhs imposed on Span Motels Pvt. Ltd for pollution in the Beas River area by the motel.

Source: Compiled from legal cases listed in *Legal and Scientific Resources for Asia*, and CSE (1999).

The most noteworthy feature of the SC rulings on industrial pollution is that the "polluter pays principle" has been adopted formally, and the industries have been given the message that the adverse environmental costs of industrial activities have to be internalized. During the Tamil Nadu tanneries case in 1996, the precautionary principle and the polluter pays principle were accepted as the *law of the land*, and stated as essential features of sustainable development. Articles 21, 47, 48A and 51A(g) of the Indian Constitution have been quoted by the SC as giving a clear mandate to the state to protect and improve the environment and safeguard the forests and wildlife of the country.

Moreover, through the rulings, the SC has induced the pollution control authority to undertake action like estimating damage cost imposed on the economy by polluting industries and recovering it (notably the Bichhri case in 1996). Much like inducing vehicular environmental norms in India, the SC asked the government to establish Coastal Management Authorities (both at the center and the state levels), that would develop policies to protect India's coastal ecosystem.

7.5 Judicial Activism: Coase vs Moral Suasion in Pollution Control

The natural question that follows from the observation of a significant number of environmental court cases during the 1990s (and a few post-2000) is, how important a role has public interest litigation really played in the pollution management regime in India?

First, the instances of court rulings in both vehicular pollution and industrial pollution cases discussed above indicate that important legislation was initiated in India, especially in terms of vehicular emission standards, that did not exist earlier. Thus, the community (as represented by individuals or NGOs) has helped in bringing about institutional changes in terms of sectors covered by environmental legislation, besides being informal regulators.

Second, while in India, Coase-style negotiations have not taken place, as in some other countries like Indonesia (Pargal and Wheeler 1995), the environmental cases have brought polluters to court to pay for the damages/social costs imposed on society. Indeed, most of the public interest litigations have typically been those involving large numbers (of polluters and victims), i.e. the pollution cases involved a large number of dispersed polluters (e.g. SSIs in Delhi, or leather tanneries in Kolkata and Kanpur, or mobile polluters like vehicles), as well as a large number of victims (the urban population), where Coasian negotiations would not have been feasible due to high transaction costs.

Third, the equity issue, which poses a major challenge in any pollution control strategy, has been dealt with quite clearly in the Supreme Court rulings. While recognizing the hardship of industrial units going out of business, a Supreme Court ruling against polluting units noted that, "it is a price that has to be paid for protecting and safeguarding the right of the people living in a healthy environment with minimal disturbance of ecological balance and without avoidable hazard to them, their cattle, homes and agriculture and undue affectation of air water and environment."[16] This reflects, in essence, the objective of environmental management programs – namely that of allocating resources for production and consumption according to their true social costs. The "purpose is to achieve important targets for environmental quality... where their adverse redistributional impact can be easily addressed, it is surely important to do so, but *environmental measures should not, in general be side-tracked on redistributional grounds.*" (emphasis added, Oates 1994: 129)

Yet, the scope of the judicial approach to achieve the optimal pollution equilibrium with the property rights defined in favor of the victims (given that the Supreme Court rulings have endorsed the polluter pays principle), is limited. In reality, even the orders of the Supreme Court have sometimes not been implemented! Indeed, a pure judicial approach to pollution abatement can never be economically efficient or effective,[17] since judicial procedures can always be used for stalling remedial action. For example, following the 1996 Supreme Court closure notice, 168 hazardous industrial units in Delhi across residential areas should have closed down (*M.C. Mehta v. India* case).[18] Yet, even three years after the court order, the affected industries succeeded in stalling the process by court appeals. Some industries (including Birla Textile Mills and Swantantra Bharat Mills) appealed that the order violated their fundamental rights based on existing laws, like the Delhi Development Act, the Industrial Disputes Act and the Minimum Wages Act, on the issue of compensation to displaced industry and workers. The industry's writ petition also questioned the authority of the Supreme Court to declare surrendered land as green areas.[19]

According to the SC ruling, the workers of the industries were to be employed in the new location or be retrenched: wages were to be paid for the shifting period as well as one year's wages as shifting bonus, and those workers who chose not to relocate were to be considered as retrenched. After relocation, however, companies could not absorb all the employees by the date specified. In one case, the SC then asked the firm to absorb the number of employees it could and continue to give shifting allowance to the others as per the original order.[20]

The above instance highlights the inevitable drawback of a judiciary regime of pollution control in an economy: namely, the thorny issues of relocation and employment may be pitched as imposing unnecessary social costs and thereby pollution is always viewed as a trade-off against higher economic growth and employment. A pure judicial approach also allows polluting firms to resort to legal mechanisms and obtain stay orders against closure/shifting decisions of the judiciary, and to stall action for years.

Judicial activism, however, has accomplished something else. It has given a clear market signal that the polluting activities of industry will not be tolerated, and the damage costs are far too large to be ignored by the community. In effect, PILs have acted as what the literature terms an indirect market-based instrument, and can be classified as a *suasive instrument* (moral suasion instrument). Typically, suasive instruments include environmental education or information that can alter the behavioral pattern of polluters, including public disclosure of information on polluting activities of industries, which creates market pressure on manufacturers to adopt environmentally friendly production processes or produce greener products. The court rulings by endorsing the polluter pays principle, have sent a clear signal to polluters that they now have to pay up for the environmental and health damages they impose on society.

As an indirect market-based instrument, judicial activism in India imparts the message that dumping of wastes into the ecosystem is no longer costless for the polluters. In fact, even when implementation of judicial orders is stalled in the appeals court by the polluters, it entails costs (in terms of time, lost income and court fees) on the polluters. Besides monetary costs, bigger corporations like to minimize the risk of an environmental litigation, which can damage their reputation seriously in the marketplace. To ensure positive publicity, the increase in judicial activism induces larger companies to undertake pollution control measures.

The fact that public interest litigation and judicial activism have had distinct market implications is borne out by the growth of the domestic environment industry and the signal it has given to foreign investors. Indeed the *US Country Commercial Guide (USDOC 2002)* to invest in India for potential US investors noted that environmental judicial activism is an important factor aiding the growth of the environment market (discussed in the previous chapter) in India. Thus, while direct market-based instruments for pollution control remain in the pipeline, public interest environmental litigations in the last decade have succeeded in transmitting indirect market signals to the industry to internalize environmental costs.

Table 7A.1 Indian and International Ambient Air Quality Standards ($\mu g/m^3$)
(Annual Average Standards)

Pollutant	India (1994)			WHO (1999)	USEPA (1997)	UK (1997)
	Industrial	Residential	Sensitive			
Nitrogen oxides	80	60	15	40	100	21ppb
Sulfur dioxide	80	60	15	50	80	100ppb[a]
Carbon monoxide[b]	5000	2000	1000	10000	10000	10ppm
Lead	1	0.75	0.50	0.5	1.5	0.5
PM_{10} Annual	120	60	50	-	50	-
24-hourly	150	100	75	-	150	50
SPM	360	140	70	-	-	-

[a] Refers to 15-minute average standard, not annual average.
[b] Carbon monoxide standards are 8 hourly standards, not the annual average; SPM = suspended particulate matter, PM_{10} = particles with aerodynamic diameter 10 μm or less (respirable SPM).
ppb = parts per billion, ppm= parts per million.

Source: Selected from data in Table 5.1, CPCB (2000).

Table 7A.2 SPM Levels (μg/m³) in Five Most Populous Indian Cities, 1990-1998

City	Area	1990	1991	1992	1993	1994	1995	1996	1997	1998
Mumbai	R	211	267	283	238	209	233	196	327	103
	I	180	199	150	227	276	271	247	240	226
Delhi	R	317	300	351	358	385	409	371	365	341
	I	381	349	431	402	362	403	420	314	367
Kolkata	R	205	338	304	317	326	308	491	-	275
	I	302	496	313	640	476	447	514	-	286
Bangalore	R	68	60	-	-	-	-	199	222	239
	I	109	99	-	-	-	-	130	153	134
Chennai	R	109	118	85	72	104	106	84	101	116
	I	129	147	53	121	146	142	136	111	126

R = residential area, I = industrial area.

Source: Selected data from CPCB (2000) *Air Quality Status and Trends in India* (Table 6.3 and Table 6.9).

Table 7A.3 Vehicular Emission Load in Five Indian Metropolitan Cities, 1996 (tons per day)

City \ Pollutant	Particulate	SO₂	NOₓ	HC	CO	Total
Mumbai	5.59	4.03	70.82	108.21	469.92	659.57
Delhi	10.30	8.96	126.46	249.57	651.01	1046.30
Kolkata	3.25	3.65	54.69	43.88	188.24	239.71
Bangalore	2.62	1.76	26.22	78.51	195.36	304.47
Chennai	2.34	2.02	28.21	50.46	143.22	226.25

SO_2 = sulfur dioxide, NO_x = Nitrogen oxides, HC = hydrocarbon, CO = carbon monoxide.

Source: TERI Urban Transport and Environment Statistics, reprinted from Central Pollution Control Board, New Delhi "Urban Statistics", October 1996.

Table 7A.4 Bharat Stage II Emission Standards (gms/kms), 2000

Vehicle with:	CO (g/kms)	HC &NO$_x$ (g/kms)	PM (g/kms)
Gasoline engine			
GVW< 2.5 tons	2.2	0.5	-
2.5< GVW < 3.5 tons	2.2 - 5	0.5 - 0.7	-
Diesel engine			
GVW < 2.5 tons	1.0	0.7	0.08
2.5< GVW < 3.5 tons	1.0 - 1.5	0.7 - 1.2	0.08 - 0.17
GVW > 3.5 tons	4.0	1.1 & 7.0*	0.15

* 1.1 g/kmh for HC and 7.0 g/kmh for NOx respectively.
CO = carbon monoxide, HC = hydrocarbon, NO$_x$ = nitrogen oxide, PM = particulate matter.

Notes

[1] How much compensation any party pays depends on the bargaining power of the two.
[2] The paper however reported that in the sample of 250 Indian plants, 102 plants indicated that abatement had been undertaken in response to complaints from neighboring communities, and 51 plants had done so in response to NGO pressure (Pargal, Mani and Huq 1997: 6).
[3] This leads to high damage costs particularly in the case of stock pollutants (where absorptive capacity of the environmental resource medium is limited), like chemical contamination of water.
[4] A polluter has an incentive to abide by the environmental standards, only if the marginal cost of offense is greater than the marginal benefit from violation. The marginal cost of offense is determined by the product of the probability of detection times the probability of prosecution (given detection) times probability of conviction (given prosecution) times the fine (Bowers 1997: 66). As long as the probability of detection and conviction remain low in India, the command-and-control approach to pollution control will fail to induce potential polluters to abate.
[5] It should be noted, however, that given the political and technological constraints sometimes CAC measures are better suited than economic instruments for certain pollution problems (Hahn and Stavins 1992: 465). For example, when pollution is highly localized, with threshold/non-linear damage functions, source-specific standards may be more appropriate. Economic instruments are particularly desirable when pollution is uniformly mixed over large geographical areas.
[6] The distinction between reactionary and progressive judicial activism has been made by Professor Upendra Baxi in the preface of Sathe (2002).
[7] *T.N. Godavaram Thirumulpad v. India* (1997) 2 SCC 267 in protection and conservation of forests; *M.C. Mehta v. India* (1997) 3 SCC715 for protection and conservation of wildlife; *Almitrah Patel v. India* (1998) 2 SCC 416 for urban and solid waste management. Sathe (2002): 224.
[8] "Deadly Particles", *Down To Earth*, December 15, 1999.

[9] Monitoring data over the last decade indicates that 6,086 kms of river stretches are highly polluted (BOD>6mg/litre), 8,691 kms moderately polluted (BOD = 3-6mg/litre) and 30,242 kms relatively clean (BOD, 3 mg/liter). Water quality monitoring was started in 1976 and at present there are 507 stations in the country, of which 414 are on rivers, 25 on ground water, 38 on lakes and 30 on canals, creeks, drains and ponds (CPCB 2001: 28).

[10] *Economic Survey of India, 2000-01*: 207.

[11] Cropper, Simon, Alberini and Sharma (1999) "The Health Effects of Air Pollution in Delhi", World Bank.

[12] The latter has been used to grant compensation to displaced workers during closure of polluting industrial units. Another legislation, the National Environmental Tribunal Act (1995) introduced strict liability and is meant for large-scale accidents and damages involving hazardous wastes and chemicals.

[13] Central Pollution Control Board publication *Parivesh* 2001, September issue: 34.

[14] One perception is that regulatory authorities may be averse to shutting down plants since it can lead to unemployment and social unrest, while another perception is that defaulting firm owners can stop such drastic measures by using their political clout. If one were to accept the second line of argument, namely the problem of corruption, then the increasing role of public participation in pollution management is good. Public participation can be seen to have additional benefit in providing a means of dealing with the unholy nexus of industrialists and politicians, at the cost of the environment.

[15] For many SSIs even basic data on value added, turnover, employment, and capital stock is not available, let alone abatement expenditure. Since these units operate on small profit margins, the cost of non-compliance is lower than the cost of compliance (given the regulatory and monitoring structure, as well as corruption). There are fiscal incentives available for the SSIs, which are expected to help these units set up common effluent treatment plants and thereby reduce pollution from this sector.

[16] Cited in Delhi Land Use: Badkhal Lake and Surajkund (1996) from a Supreme Court ruling of Rural Litigation and Entitlement *Kendra v. State of UP* (1986, SCC 517 and 1987 SCR614) that can be said to be the harbinger of the new trend. In the latter case, the SC ordered the limestone quarries in the Mussourie Hills to be closed since they were a hazard to the environment.

[17] Advocate M.C. Mehta, the main mover of the Supreme Court rulings, admits that judicial activism is not the answer, rather it is the only tool for citizens when formal enforcement fails. Interview published in *Frontline*, Volume 17, December 9-22, 2000.

[18] Similarly closure notices, effective January 1997, were issued to 39,000 illegal small industrial units and 513 hazardous units around the city in case they failed to relocate within the allotted time. *Down to Earth*, May 15, 1997, page 28.

[19] "Slag in polluting industry ruling", *Economic Times* September 12, 1999, page 1.

[20] *Workmen of M/s Birla Textiles v. K.M. Birla* 1999, Sathe (2002): 226.

Chapter 8

Community Participation in Natural Resource Management

8.1 Whither Indian Villages?

While urban India joins the global village and environmental management of the formal sectors is influenced by international action, what is the state of environmental management in Indian villages? Today, despite increasing modernization and urbanization, the majority of the Indian population, about 70%, lives in villages, and the country's workforce is largely engaged in farming and allied activities, with 60% of the labor force engaged in agriculture, forestry and fishing today.[1] Astounding, as it may seem, the advances in technologically driven sectors like software are taking place in India while the economy remains largely agrarian!

The natural resource base of a largely agrarian economy is important for the agricultural and allied sector, as well as for direct consumption of common property resources. Since the natural resource base is intrinsically important for the livelihood of poor villagers, the rural poor have suffered from the degradation of the resource base that has taken place in the country: typically that of land, water and forestry. The overexploitation of natural resources has resulted from the absence of collective action, and conditions of poverty have further exacerbated the situation.

The renewability of resources like forestry or fishery, does not guarantee that the resources will indeed regenerate themselves, but is determined by the use pattern, and the rate of harvest. The management regime of natural resources is critical in determining the sustainability of the resources, and although extinction of a resource may turn out to be optimal based on economic modeling, it leads to a basic contradiction with the philosophy of sustainable development (Pearce and Warford 1993). In developing countries like India, the resource management regime was traditionally based on customs and laws, even in the absence of formal property titles. With the social, demographic, institutional, and economic changes that have been taking place over several decades, the historical community rules of harvesting of natural resources were affected. Some of the changes include: increasing population pressure, parceling of land into smaller holdings, break-down of older farming families due to rural-urban migration, government land reforms, greater monetization of the rural economy, etc. This chapter concentrates on the more recent attempts to evolve community partnership with government, in the management of natural resources in India.

Broadly natural resources can have four types of property regimes: open access regime, common property regime, state ownership, and private ownership (Bromley 1989, Pearce and Warford 1993). The open access regime (complete absence of property rights) typically leads to a "tragedy of the commons" (Hardin

1968) as users overexploit resources like grazing lands, fishery and forestry, since the private cost of using the resource is less than its true social cost. One solution to the commons problem is the assignment of property rights, so that owners limit the use of the commons. The common property resource regime is based on communal rules and regulations to ensure the sustainable use of resources. Indigenous communities across the globe have used such a regime and these people have been found to have extensive knowledge of soils, natural medicines, risk-minimizing cropping practices, etc (Pearce and Warford 1993: 253). Yet communal management regimes have failed in the face of institutional, economic and social changes including the demarcation of reserve forests and national parks (where access of communities for harvesting forest products are denied); population growth; and use of modern technology leading to over extraction and degradation of resources (like mechanized fishing). The collapse of the community management regime has led the way back to the tragedy of the commons.

State ownership seems to be a solution to overuse of resources, since the state can set and enforce rules for sustainable harvesting. The system, however, can work well only if the state is efficient and the rules are acceptable to the community. Similarly, private ownership of resources can solve the problem of the tragedy of the commons if the property titles are well defined. While private ownership of resources seems consistent with sustainable resource management, there could be instances where this may not be so if individual discount rates are greater than the resource regeneration rate, or external diseconomies continue, as indicated by experiences in some African countries (Pearce and Warford 1993).

In India, the natural resource management problems are analyzed in this chapter under two broad categories of resource degradation; those stemming from: (i) commercial agricultural activities, especially due to use of chemical pesticides, fertilizers, groundwater; and (ii) direct consumption of common natural resource base, including timber and other forest products.

In the agricultural sector, the degradation of the resource base, typically soil, has resulted from population pressure, agricultural policies and practices encouraged in order to increase food production. In a bid to increase food production, four decades ago the Green Revolution was embraced in India, with targeted policies encouraging the use of chemical fertilizers and pesticides, and extensive piped irrigation. This, however, led to improper use of agricultural inputs, resulting in reduced resilience of agricultural land to pests and diseases; chemical contamination of groundwater/surface water due to run-off, human health problems due to chemical residues in food, and decline in the water table due to over extraction of ground water for irrigation.[2]

The common property resources (CPRs) like forests, pasture lands, and waterways have suffered degradation due to population growth, commercialization of the village economy and the erosion of traditional resource management practices. Population pressure has also forced forest clearing for construction and agriculture, and poverty is also believed to have led to higher future discount rates of the poorer households to ensure present sustenance.

The preservation of natural resources is crucial not only to sustain and improve agricultural, forestry and fisheries production, but also to protect the rich biological diversity of the country. Moreover, the daily sustenance of the rural poor, typically landless laborers and marginal farmers (with smallholdings), depends on CPRs for most of their consumption – thus any improvement in common property resources is beneficial for the rural poor. Indeed, the Indian environmentalist, the late Anil Agarwal had interpreted the challenge of *economic poverty* in the country as that of *ecological poverty*. He had supported the promotion of community-based natural resource management on a larger scale to help wipe out a substantial part of India's rural poverty (given the indigenous communities' traditional resource management knowledge).

Changes in global markets in the last decade have also impacted natural resource management in India. For example, the demand for organic food in the global market has provided an incentive to re-evaluate and encourage the long-term merits of traditional Indian organic farming and sustainable agricultural practices. Moreover, the traditional knowledge system of the use of medicinal plants in India has gained significant market price in the global economy, since India is one of the biodiversity rich countries of the world, and has encouraged their documentation and registration (see the next chapter).

8.2 Development and Indian Rural Society

In a large populous country like India, environmental degradation of the CPRs is typically associated with population pressure and poverty of the rural masses. Economists have suggested that "control of population growth would probably be the best available policy on behalf of sustainability" (Solow 1993). The process of development by itself can play an important role in sustainability through its effect on reducing fertility rate, and alleviation of poverty.

Table 8.1 highlights some of the socio-development indicators in rural India as compared to the urban sector, in the last two decades. In particular, education, one of the most important determinants of population growth, has been increasing, and today 80% of urban and close to 60% of rural India is literate. Moreover, female literacy increased from 39% in 1991 to 54% in 2001. This is important since female literacy has earlier been shown to have a negative and highly significant effect on fertility (Dreze and Murthi 2000). The current trend in female literacy suggests that this will help reduce population growth and eventually arrest the population pressure on the country's environmental resources.

The problem of deforestation in India has also been aggravated due to population growth, economic and technological changes. Village level household survey and forest cover data over 29 years, during the period 1971 through 1999, has shown that higher population growth and agricultural technical change led to reduced forest area and density. Agricultural technical change, while increasing productivity growth (Green Revolution) and income (which reduces villagers' biomass dependence on forests), also increased rent of arable land and reinforced deforestation. Thus, income growth affected deforestation through its effect on the opportunity costs of land use. At the same time, the data indicates that economic growth (increased income) and increased demand for forest products led to forest growth in these villages (Foster and Rosenzweig 2002).

Table 8.1 Selected Developmental Indicators of India, 1981-2001

Indicator	1981	1991	2001
Literacy rate	43.6	52.2	65.4
Rural	36.0	44.7	59.4
Urban	67.2	73.1	80.3
Fertility rate (per woman)	4.5	3.6	3.2[a]
Rural	4.8	3.9	-
Urban	3.3	2.7	-
Poverty (% population below poverty line)[b]	44.5	38.9	36.0
Rural	45.7	39.1	37.3
Urban	40.8	38.2	32.4

[a]Corresponds to 1998.
[b]Poverty indicator corresponds to the years 1983, 1987-88, and 1993-94 in the three columns. More recent estimates indicate poverty to be 26% for 1999-2000 (27% for rural and 23.6% for urban), based on sample surveys in India, but these are not quite comparable to the previous years.

Source: Compiled from data reported in *Census of India 2001* and *1991; Economic Survey 2001-02; Compendium of Environment Statistics 2000 World Development Indicators 2001.*

At the aggregate level, therefore, the process of development can still have a positive environmental impact. Kumar and Aggarwal (2001) showed that during the period 1963-95, the decline in poverty seems to have had a positive environmental impact (measured by increase in forest cover or pasture land and declining crop area), in at least some of the Indian states. The study demonstrated that an inverted U-shaped environmental Kuznets curve seems to hold between income growth and forest cover for states like Punjab and Haryana.

A study on the economic and social costs of environmental degradation in India estimated that water and air pollution costs approximately US$7 billion per year, and land degradation and deforestation costs about US$2.7 billion annually (Brandon et al 1995). Economic growth can improve the quality of the environment (like sanitation, indoor and outdoor air quality) and reduce poverty and fertility (which in turn eventually have a positive effect on the environment), but it may not be able to arrest natural resource degradation. For example, this would be true in case of loss of biodiversity with deforestation and change in land use. Indigenous species of flora and fauna lost during deforestation can never be replaced, by the time the positive income effects (à la Environmental Kuznets Curve) kick in.

Sustainable economic development is considered to be achievable as long as market prices of all inputs and products reflect their true social (including environmental) costs. The latter condition seems reasonable for a well-informed, formal-transaction economy, but in an agro-economic system where the transactions are not marketed, as in rural India, it is the rules of the game in resource use (defined in terms of social relationships and behavioral norms) that matter most.

Moreover, while economic development does help eventually, the process may be accompanied by environmental degradation of the CPRs, which in turn has an adverse impact. The decline in environmental quality itself has socio-economic impacts: with degradation of natural resources, poverty increases since rural livelihood is crucially dependent on resource productivity of CPRs. This in turn leads to other problems like migration out of villages, which in turn adversely affects the community efforts to preserve the commons. Thus, to alleviate rural poverty, the natural resource base needs to be improved and output-sharing well specified. Such an approach to resource management requires local level participation.

In India, the institutional and social changes over time have broken down indigenous structures or norms that traditionally regulated resource use earlier in the country, and the government regulations for protecting natural resources like forests failed to stop over-exploitation. Neither did a centralized policy to protect common lands and forests work. Thus the Indian government began to formally adopt community participation in the management of the local commons in the late 1980s.

8.3 Environmental Degradation in the Agricultural Sector and the Green Revolution

In order to increase food production for the rapidly increasing population, in the 1960s, intensification of agriculture began with the use of chemical fertilizers and expansion of irrigation, under the Green Revolution. India aggressively promoted the use of chemical fertilizers and pesticides with high yielding varieties of seeds, in an effort to increase agricultural output to feed the rapidly growing population of the country. In 1966, new varieties of high yielding seeds (responding to greater use of chemical fertilizers) were introduced in the country during the Green Revolution.

The use of fertilizer has increased significantly in India over the last four decades. The chemical fertilizer consumption increased from 0.29 million tons in 1960-61 to 19.2 million tons in 1999-2000 (MOEF 2001: 31). Increased chemical input has in effect degraded the soil quality and also reduced the natural resilience of the agricultural sector against diseases, pest attacks and climate shocks. Moreover, improper irrigation has waterlogged or salinized millions of hectares of farmland, and also caused water tables to fall.

India thus succeeded in attaining self-sufficiency in food at the cost of a degraded ecosystem. A World Bank study estimated that the annual loss in production of 11 major crops in India is approximately 0.5-1.3 million tons due to depletion of soil nutrients, as a result of unsuitable agricultural practices (Brandon et al 1995). The loss in crop production due to salinity in India is in the range of 6.2-9.7 million tons (ibid). On the other hand, waterlogging problems, due to improper irrigation, have increased the number of breeding sites for vectors and parasites of diseases such as dengue and malaria (Repetto 1994).

8.3.1 A Greener Revolution?

A greener revolution can potentially sweep the globe with the promotion of sustainable agriculture – replacing chemicals with natural fertilizers and pesticides, and locally adapted farming practices. The survey of sustainable farming projects around the world (Pretty and Hine 2001) during the last 10-15 years showed that the gains from such agricultural practices are highest among poor farms in developing countries, including India. Besides minimizing ecological costs from agriculture (compared to chemical run-off, chemical contamination in food chain, poisoning groundwater), sustainable agriculture makes better use of indigenous knowledge and the skill of the farmers and the local community.

In the 1990s, the issue of organic agricultural inputs gained in prominence in India, with the development of an international market for organic products. Organic cultivation being labor-intensive, it is especially promising for a populous country like India. Small and scattered farming communities across India can find economic gains, e.g. Peermade Development Society (IFOAM member), an NGO in Kerala and the largest Indian exporter of organic spices, encourages production/export of organic spices from rural areas, including the tribal communities. This has provided a channel to source products from the widely dispersed small organic farming communities (which are too financially handicapped to undergo the expense of organic product certification individually) all over India. Also, the wealth of traditional knowledge in the field of natural pesticides, herbicides, and manure, can be tapped and further developed in India.

Data on the consumption of technical grade pesticides in India indicates that between 1990-91 and 1995-96, consumption decreased from 75,000 tons to 56,110 tons, due to the increased use of safer pesticides including neem-based and bio-pesticides (MOEF 2001: 32).

To increase agricultural productivity, as well as to improve natural resource management of land and water (including rainfall), participatory watershed management has been promoted in India. The watershed management programs are meant to especially help the small and marginal farmers in the drylands (where productivity is low, and agricultural income often supplemented by employment outside their own farms), and promise agricultural development, employment generation and poverty alleviation. The participatory approach to watershed management and degraded lands initiated in India will be taken up later in this chapter.

8.3.2 Role and Management of Common Property Resources in India

The rural poor in India, including the landless laborers and marginal farmers, depend on common property resources for most of their consumption needs of food, fuel and fodder. Several village level studies have estimated that the contribution of common property resources (CPRs) ranges from 12 to 25% in poor rural household income, and the poorer the household, the greater is the importance of income derived from CPRs (Beck and Nesmith, 2001). Moreover, despite the degradation and reduced productivity, CPRs continue to provide a significant proportion of household income, and the gathering of fuel, fodder and water continues to constitute the daily routine of almost all village households. Besides food, fodder and fuel, rural households (typically women and children) also collect medicinal plants, building materials and materials for household items and farm implements from the forests.

There are specific gender issues associated with the management of CPRs. Women, in particular, play an important role in the management of natural resources, since they are the major gatherers and users of a wide range of non-timber forest products. Degradation of CPRs affects women (and children) adversely; for example, deforestation increases the time and distance involved in grazing and collection of fuel and food. Moreover, the reduced – or non-availability of non-timber forest products has changed occupational patterns of women from self-employment to wage employment.

Traditionally, natural resources have always had close social ties with Indian village life. The use of CPRs 'has been' *or* 'is' associated with several community customs, which basically ensured that the CPR harvesting was sustainable (giving time for regeneration), and that resources were shared among the villagers. Village communities even maintained "sacred groves" where harvest of timber or forest products was banned or restricted. These sacred groves were small patches of native vegetation (sizes varied from less than a hectare to more than a few hundred hectares). This traditional practice (often in the name of some local deity) helped conserve and enhance biological diversity in the local ecosystem. Several small sacred groves in the southern state of Kerala are rich in biological diversity, and resemble the typical spectrum of a tropical forest (CEE, 2002). Such a system could work as long as population pressure was not high, and there was social sanction of the community rules and practices.

Over the years, the rural sector has experienced social and institutional changes that have affected the management of CPRs. Increase in population pressure coupled with poverty, integration with the market, and change in farming practices, eroded the traditional social and institutional framework that protected and regulated the use of CPRs. Jodha (1995) identified rural transformation as the key factor affecting the status of CPRs, which has either reduced the importance of CPRs in the rural economy, or has made it difficult to maintain them as dependable community assets. The process of transformation included increased technological and institutional interventions by the state, change in farming practices, greater market integration, increased population pressure and significant changes in people's attitude towards common resources. For instance, increased irrigation facility and tractorization, increase in land prices, and opportunity for privatization of land, created incentives to reduce CPR area. Indeed the CPR areas declined by 31-55% during 1950-1980 in 82 villages across seven Indian states (Jodha 1990).

Since the process of economic development cannot automatically ensure the sustainable use of natural resources (particularly CPRs), a sound management system for natural resources is essential. To be effective, the resource management systems must be acceptable to the local populations, i.e. community participation is vital for the system to be robust. A study on the effectiveness of local level intervention on economic and demographic variables in the district of Udaipur, Rajasthan (Chopra and Gulati 1998) found that stress migration from the rural areas decreased and possibly reversed due to the introduction of better management of common property resources in these areas.

8.4 Community Participation in CPR Management

The traditional Indian rural community had integrated nature into culture such that harvest and consumption habits as well as cultural events built in ecological factors like regeneration of different species of plants and animals. Over time, however, the rural society changed, and CPRs faced unregulated exploitation. As the environmental sociologist Ramchandra Guha observed, it is too simplistic to expect village communities today to manage natural resources sustainably by themselves, since values and incentives have changed with the growth of individualism. For instance, there is a greater market for forest produce, and hence greater incentive for influential individuals to break customary sanctions. A partnership between the state and local community seems more promising.

The failure of both the traditional and centralized systems of natural resources regulation to arrest the degradation of CPRs, prompted the Indian Government to promote a community-based government management of ecological resources, especially in watershed areas and forests. The model of community-based conservation of natural resources comprises of the local population in partnership with the government, or NGOs, or international agencies, or a combination of all three. A study (Agrawal and Yadama, 1997) in the Himalayan forest region of Kumaon in India, estimated the relative effects of population, market and institutional pressures on resource use. A key finding of the study indicated that local institutions created by the state play a critical role in mediating the influence of structural and socio-economic variables.

Certain conditions, however, are necessary for an effective local level participatory management of natural resources. Considering participatory management as a cooperative game, built-in incentives and disincentives are crucial in determining whether the members will cooperate or not. To obtain a coalition outcome (or equilibrium), the relevant factors determining the payoff to the players must be beyond certain threshold values. The functioning of the local level institutions are thus significant in determining whether the social norms set in the participatory management system are effective to ensure the cooperative outcome (Sethi and Somanathan 1996). The efficacy of social sanctions however can be adversely affected with incursion of outsiders or of outside interests through the operation of market forces that can lead to a breakdown of the cooperative norm (ibid). The final success of participatory management so far in India (discussed later in this section) has been determined by the extent of true involvement of the local community in decision-making, and cost and benefit sharing of the CPRs.

Independent non-governmental efforts had earlier successfully experimented with community-based resource management in villages in the 1980s. The merits of community-based resource management prompted the Indian Government also to formally adopt this approach; however, in reality, the approach has been more of community "participatory" resource management, rather than being completely managed by the community. Moreover, only two sectors of forestry and watershed (and irrigation) management have such community programs.

The state-initiated Joint Forest Management (JFM) program was launched in 1990. In the JFM, villagers and government share the responsibility and benefits (harvest of wood and non-timber forest products) of regenerating degraded local forests (defined by low vegetation cover). Through the 73rd Constitutional Amendment in 1992, the government empowered Panchayat (local level) bodies and made them responsible for soil conservation, water management watershed development, social and farm forestry, drinking water, non-conventional energy sources, and maintenance of community assets. In 1994, the Indian Government also issued guidelines for watershed development, which became an integral part of rural development.

The following sections discuss the environmental management of CPRs, in particular community participation in watershed development programs and joint forest management, which are aimed at a broader goal of harmonizing the use of several natural resources, including water, soil, forest and pasture lands.

8.4.1 Experience with Participatory Watershed Management

Community participation in watershed management was first launched in the mid-1980s under the National Watershed Development Program for Rainfed Agriculture. Considering the significant role of women in the rural economy, the 1994 Watershed Guidelines emphasized greater participation of women and marginal groups. Watershed management is especially important since large tracts of degraded land in India are classified as CPRs, and today watershed management projects to increase agricultural productivity have become an integral part of rural development programs. Evaluation studies of participatory watershed management projects in India have identified some key conditions that have made the difference between success and failure.

A review of 36 watershed projects across the five Indian states of Andhra Pradesh, Karnataka, Maharashtra, Orissa and Rajasthan, identified the characteristics essential for mainstreaming sustainable watershed management in the country (Kolavalli and Kerr 2002). The study distinguished between four types of projects: government-funded and implemented; multilateral/bilateral-funded and government-implemented; jointly implemented with NGOs; and NGO-implemented. The project analyses were based on three aspects of implementation: social organization, joint decision-making and cost sharing. Only those projects that had social organization with a fair representation of village participants, high level of local decision-making, and cost-sharing with farmers emerged successful. NGO-implemented projects scored high on account of all three aspects. The study indicated three characteristics that were important in determining the success of participatory watershed management projects:

(i) choosing a village rather than a watershed spanning several villages as the basis for operation; (ii) consensus-based decision-making that involved locals, versus centralized decision-making; (iii) sharing costs with farmers to increase their stake in the project, as well as to reduce the overall costs of the project.

(i) First, choosing a village as the basis of project operation (rather than a watershed that spans multiple villages) facilitated the communication among the project stakeholders (avoiding negotiations of cost and benefit sharing across villages). All NGO projects (except one), with a higher success rate, chose a village or watershed within a village as the unit of operation, while most government-implemented projects chose a watershed as the unit of operation (spanning villages).

(ii) Second, decisions based on consensus of the locals (true people's participation) compared to more centralized decisions, was a distinguishing feature of the NGO-implemented projects, and were more effective in the execution of decisions. For instance, farmers were found to prefer conservation measures that also enhanced productivity in the short run, and the planting of trees in private lands (which factored in their concerns on returns), as opposed to technocrats emphasizing productivity of common lands, and planting trees in common lands. Thus, when farmers' priorities were incorporated, the community involvement increased in the watershed programs.

(iii) Third, projects with cost sharing, where farmers contributed to the cost of the watershed program, were more successful, since it increased the stake for the local community. The jointly implemented and NGO-implemented projects had made more efforts in sharing costs with the locals, and typically 10 to 30% of the costs were borne by farmers. On the other hand, government-implemented projects had zero or marginal costs being borne by the farmers. Cost sharing was identified as an important factor which reduced the bureaucracy's control over projects, and made the process more transparent (and subject to community scrutiny). It was also observed that the maintenance of soil and water conservation investments on private rainfed land in the states of Andhra Pradesh and Maharashtra increased steadily in proportion with the percentage cost borne by the farmer (Kerr et al 2000).

Thus, when the village community is involved as a stakeholder in CPR management in the complete sense of the term, namely participants are clearly defined (within a village), decision-making is based on consensus, and when villagers share the costs (besides benefits), programs have worked effectively. However, as in any environmental program, equity issues are just as contentious in these programs. For instance, analysts have been critical of the fact that watershed development programs seem to benefit landed farmers (through increase in agricultural productivity) rather than the relatively poor landless villagers. There are instances where the design of the watershed project adversely affected the rural poor: for example, in the state of Maharashtra, shepherds suffered when the common access lands that provided grazing grounds for their animals were sealed off during the re-vegetation phase of the watershed projects (Kerr et al 2000). Even after regeneration the restrictions on grazing had not been lifted, and the employment generation in the projects did not compensate for this loss of access to common lands. This, however, was not the case with NGO-implemented projects, which performed the best, since community participation and priorities were incorporated to a much larger extent.

8.4.2 Experience with Participatory Forest Management

India's forest management policy has a two-pronged approach: first, creation of reserved areas; and second, involvement of people in collective management of forests. National parks and wildlife sanctuaries have been created as protected areas under the Wildlife Protection Act (1972), and today there are 87 national parks and 484 wildlife sanctuaries, with total areas of 4.06 million hectares and 11.54 million hectares respectively (totaling 15.6 million hectares or 4.74% of the geographic area of India). While there is no provision for community participation in wildlife resource management, the story is quite different in forest management.

Village participation in forest management was earlier defined in the 1927 Indian Forest Act, in the chapter on *Village Forests*. The management of the village forests, however, was regulated by the government, as evident from the text of the legislation. Thus the provision of the 1927 Act cannot be considered to be a participatory management regime in the true sense of the term.

> The State Government may assign to any village-community the rights of government to or over any land which has been constituted a reserved forest, and may cancel such assignment. All forests so assigned shall be called village-forests.
>
> The State Government may make rules for regulating the management of village-forests, prescribing the conditions under which the community to which any such assignment is made may be provided with timber or other forest-produce or pasture, and their duties for the protection and improvement of such forest.
> *(Indian Forest Act, 1927, Chapter 3, section 28, paragraph 1 and 2).*

Participatory forest management, in the sense understood today in India, began in the states of West Bengal and Haryana.[3] In 1971-72 a Forest Department silviculturist in West Bengal started the initial experiment at Arabari in the Midnapore District. He was conducting some silviculture trials that were getting continuously disrupted due to fuel wood extraction or grazing by the local people. Since coercive means, through fines and arrests, failed to keep people out of the forests, he decided to try out a cooperative approach. He discussed his problem with the people and offered them some incentives in return for protection of the forest. The incentives included a share in the final crop and also gestures like flexible working hours for the local women working as laborers with the Forest Department. The local community was organized into a Forest Protection Committee (FPC) to protect the forest from illegal harvesting, overgrazing, fires and encroachment. The experiment proved to be a success and the degraded *sal* (Shorea robusta) forests of the area regenerated rapidly on being given a rest from incessant lopping and grazing. Consequently, it was extended to other parts of the State as well.[4]

The 1988 National Forest Policy envisaged people's involvement in the development and protection of forests, while meeting their livelihood needs. The principal aim of the Forest Policy was to "ensure environmental stability and maintain ecological balance", while "derivation of direct economic benefit was subordinated to this principle aim" (paragraph 2.2 of the Policy). It however, envisioned

> creating a massive people's movement with the involvement of women, for achieving these objectives and to minimise pressure on existing forests
> *(Objective 2.1, National Forest Policy 1988)*

To prevent unsustainable harvest of forests, it was recognized that providing sufficient fodder, fuel and pasture to the local population adjoining the forests was an important component of the management system. Moreover, since fuel wood continues to be the predominant source of energy in rural areas, the program of afforestation had to be intensified with special emphasis on augmenting fuel wood production to meet the requirement of the rural people. The development of tree planting and fodder resources was to be taken up in the village and community lands not required for other productive uses.[5] According to the policy, the government was to provide technical assistance and other inputs necessary for initiating such programs. Finally, the revenues generated through such programs were to accrue to the *panchayats* (local government body, in cases where the lands belonged to them), or be shared with the local communities in order to provide an incentive to them. The weaker sections, in particular, including landless labor, small and marginal farmers, tribals, and women, could be the beneficiaries entitled to the usufruct of resources like trees in return for their security and maintenance.

In June 1990, the Joint Forest Management (JFM) Program was adopted, wherein the local community would partake in resource management to regenerate *degraded* forests (defined by crown cover). There are, however, exceptions in the states of Madhya Pradesh and Chattisgarh, where non-degraded forest lands have also come under the JFM. The new guidelines on JFM indicate that the program needs to be extended to good forest areas, since one need not wait for forests to be degraded before participatory management begins (Saigal 2001: 7).

Under the JFM, forest officials and villagers agree to jointly manage the forest land surrounding the village, i.e. share both responsibilities and benefits. The process of participation between the state forest department officials and the villagers is executed through formal groups called Forest Protection Committees, which then draw up the detailed plans for the management requirements of the allotted adjoining forest area. Thus, the forest department retains the property rights to the forest area, and only a demarcated degraded forest area is allotted for JFM, where the village community is given the opportunity to execute management.

Just as in the participatory watershed management programmes, JFM programmes have also involved NGOs. NGO involvement, however, is significantly different across the states in India. While NGO participation has been limited in the states of West Bengal and Himachal Pradesh, in the southern state of Andhra Pradesh more than 250 NGOs are involved in JFM (Saigal 2001).

The JFM seems to be well rooted in a state like West Bengal and expanding in Andhra Pradesh and Madhya Pradesh. The movement of community participation spread to other regions of the country. Today over 14.25 million hectares of forest land in the country are being managed and protected by 62,890 JFM Committees across 27 states (see Table 8.2 for JFM across the states).

Today, the JFM programs cover more than 18% of total Indian forest land (Saigal 2001). These JFM programs have helped in generating income and in the increase of timber and non-timber forest products in the villages. There is also evidence that the condition of forests has improved in certain areas: in Andhra Pradesh, dense and open forests increased by 18% and 22% respectively between 1996-99 (ibid). In the state of Gujarat too, studies in the district of Sabarkantha, found that JFM programs increased the area under dense forest in eight out of ten villages studies, and the net increase was about 25%. JFM also succeeded in reducing forest encroachment in the states of Andhra Pradesh and Maharashtra. In

Andhra Pradesh about 12% of encroached land (38,158 hectares) has reportedly been vacated after the JFM program (ibid).

Table 8.2 Joint Forest Management in Indian States, 2001

State/ Union Territories	Number of JFM Committees	Area under JFM (000 hectares)	Number of families participating
Andhra Pradesh	7606	1679.1	659,305
Arunachal Pradesh	13	5.8	766
Assam	245	6.9	4,674
Bihar	296	504.6	-
Chattisgarh	6412	3391.3	471,522
Goa	26	13.0	336
Gujarat	1237	138.0	106,509
Haryana	471	65.9	9,562
Himachal Pradesh	914	111.2	45,230
Jammu & Kashmir	1895	79.5	-
Jharkhand	1379	430.5	-
Karnataka	2620	185.0	69,600
Kerala	32	4.9	3,622
Madhya Pradesh	9203	4125.8	865,902
Maharashtra	2153	686.7	102,503
Manipur	58	10.5	-
Mizoram	129	12.7	-
Nagaland	55	150.0	550
Orissa	12317	783.5	-
Punjab	188	97.2	9,366
Rajasthan	3042	309.3	272,498
Sikkim	158	0.6	3,268
Tamil Nadu	799	299.4	147,820
Tripura	160	23.5	8,303
Uttar Pradesh	502	45.0	-
Uttaranchal	7435	606.6	-
West Bengal	3545	488.1	-
Total	62,890	14,254.8	2,781,336

Source: JFM Cell, Ministry of Environment and Forests. The data pertains to June 2001.
Resources for Participatory Forestry in India website http://www.rupfor.org.

Prior to the JFM program, there had been other efforts, like Social Forestry launched in the late 1970s, to manage forest lands while taking care of the dependence of rural livelihood on forests. Under Social Forestry, massive tree planting programs were undertaken in different states to ease the pressure of rural population on government forests, by growing fuel wood, fodder and small-timber for local community needs outside the forests on village commons and private farmlands. Under the Social Forestry program, 16.57 million hectares of land were covered between 1980-81 to 1994-95, but it failed to ease the pressure on the forests, and forest degradation continued (Saigal 2001). The essential difference between Social Forestry and JFM is that, while the former sought to keep people out of the forests, the latter seeks to involve them in the management of forest lands.

Today there is still skepticism about the "participatory" nature of JFM, as to how much of real management power is invested in the villagers, and whether the state forest departments truly take on only a monitoring/technical advisory role (Lele 2000). Moreover, critics argue that the decentralization is only in terms of resource use, not property rights towards the community, since the forest department continues to have ownership of more than 95% of the forests in India. Even in the usufruct rights of forests, the state forest departments have retained substantial power, for example, in the sale of timber. This experience, however, is not uniform. The success stories in some villages also reflect greater village participation in those areas. Moreover, no matter how limited the decentralization of forest management has been in the JFM programs, there is certainly evidence that participatory management is expanding throughout the country. Perhaps the most significant feature of the JFM program is that it has paved the way towards greater participation, transparency and accountability of natural resource management in CPRs in India.

8.5 Significance of Community Participation in Resource Management

Despite the disappointments in its execution, participatory management of CPRs seems promising in India. Given the population pressure and persistence of poverty, the participatory management approach seeks to combine the local village-stakeholders' interest (as well as their indigenous knowledge) with support from the state. While the old traditional sustainable management of village commons has eroded, this is an attempt to evolve a guided re-establishment of the harmony existing between village livelihood and nature.

The involvement of the community is important, since preservation of nature is embedded in the Indian psyche, as is evident from the historical practice of maintaining sacred groves. Indeed, a noted Indian environmental scientist, Professor Madhav Gadgil observed that it is this deep-rooted tradition that is responsible for the survival of some of the last remnants of primeval vegetation in an otherwise devastated landscape, for example in the Western Ghats (Gadgil 2001: 202).

All in all, the decade of the 1990s has been a period marked by significant change in government attitudes towards the management of CPRs. How good or fair the guidance is, will remain an open question. The more important issue is that a serious effort began in the last decade to develop such an environmental resource management system, which is robust to demographic, economic and social changes in the rural economy. It has tried to replace the older centralized institutional structure towards a more community-based system. Though rudimentary and far from perfect, this seems to be a step in the right direction. Community participation is set to increase in the coming years and will hopefully correct the inadequacies of the centralized management policies followed earlier.

Notes

[1]   Compared to 76% in 1961, and 63.8% in 1993-94. The employment trend over the 1990s in India indicates that the share as well as the absolute number of workers in agriculture and allied activities declined (by 2 million workers equally divided between the urban and rural areas). Skilled professionals including technical, administrative, executive and managerial workers comprised less than 7% of the workforce during 1999-2000 (Sundaram 2001).

[2]   The government subsidizes electricity to help farmers irrigate their fields using groundwater, which has encouraged reliance on groundwater versus other sources of water.

[3]   In Haryana, one of the most prominent cases is found in Sukhomarji village where the initiative of one man led the community to rehabilitate the degraded hills, plant grass and control grazing, which led to a dramatic increase in grass productivity.

[4]   *JFM in India* in www.rupfor.org/jfm_india01.htm.

[5]   Paragraph 4.2.3, National Forest Policy 1988.

Chapter 9

Environmental Information in the Information Age

9.1 Recognition of Environmental Education and Information in India

Information and knowledge are perhaps the most powerful tools in changing behavior – be it economic, regulatory or social. Knowledge of adverse environmental effects of goods or polluting practices of firms can induce consumers to change their purchase behavior away from the polluting products or firms, and force producers to environmentally upgrade production. Similarly, knowledge of the ecological damage created in consumption can induce consumers to opt for less damaging alternatives. An environmentally educated society can also directly induce its government to administer ecologically sensitive policies.[1] Indeed, the class of indirect market-based instruments for pollution control of moral suasion (discussed in Chapter 7) is based on the increasing environmental information and awareness in the society. Thus in India, where moral suasion and community participation in environmental management have been increasing, the level of environmental information is one of the key determinants of the efficacy, such as the indirect market measure.

Environmental information, however, can be appreciated and used by only an environmentally educated society. In the last decade a drive to educate future Indian generations began by making environmental education part of the core curriculum in primary and secondary schools. This followed from the public interest writ petition filed in the Supreme Court in 1991, which sought directives to include environmental broadcast from the media as well as environmental education under Article 32 of the Constitution. The Writ Petition in particular requested the Court to:

> issue appropriate directions to cinema exhibition halls to exhibit slides containing information and messages on environment, free of cost; directions for spread of information relating to environment in national and regional languages and for broadcast thereof on the All India Radio and exposure thereof on the television in regular and short-term programs with a view to educating the people of India about their social obligation in the matter of the upkeep of the environment in proper shape and making them alive to their obligation not to act as polluting agencies or factors. There is also a prayer that environment should be made a compulsory subject in schools and colleges in a graded system so that there would be a general growth of awareness.
>
> *(Mehta v. Union of India, Environmental Education Case Supreme Court WP 860/1991)*

Consequently, in November 1991, the Supreme Court ordered cinema halls to exhibit slides on environment and pollution, and national and state television channels telecast environmental programs, on a mandatory basis. The Court also ordered all state governments and educational boards concerned with education up to the high school level in the country, to enforce environmental education beginning the next academic year (from the issue of the court order).[2]

Globalization has also played a role in highlighting the importance of environmental information and keeping formal records of the environmental wealth of the country, especially of biological diversity and traditional knowledge. As globalization began to put a price tag on the wealth of species endowment (gene pool) and the knowledge of their uses (e.g. medicinal properties of plants) that previously had been free, in India there was a realization that a formal record of environmental information was essential.

India is one of the 12 megadiversity countries of the world,[3] and the commercial use of biological resources in the world market (for example the patents on the properties of bitter gourd, neem and turmeric) induced a change in attitudes in India. It was time that the traditional knowledge held by the indigenous local communities, with regard to conservation and sustainable use of biological resources, be protected, for ensuring gains to the local population. Of course, the attempt at formalizing the indigenous knowledge is part of the exercise prescribed to signatory governments (India being one) of the 1992 Convention on Biological Diversity. The Convention recognized the significance of traditional knowledge on biodiversity held by indigenous local communities and encouraged the governments to preserve and maintain such knowledge and innovations.[4] On the other hand, the WTO Agreement on the Trade Related Intellectual Property Rights encouraged the compilation of data or other material in machine-readable form to constitute intellectual creations for protection (TRIPS Article 10). The provisions of these two multilateral agreements encouraged the compilation of traditional knowledge in India. The record of traditional Indian farming practices and innovations is also likely to be valuable in developing sustainable agriculture around the world.

9.2 Government and Non-government Activities

In terms of information on environmental pollution, India is one of the few developing countries with a network of air pollution and water pollution monitoring stations, whose readings are annually published. The installation of pollution control equipment in pollution-intensive industries is also available. Indian government offices and affiliated institutions have begun to provide information on the internet. Indeed the internet is seen as a powerful media of information dissemination, and references are made in India to a *digitally oriented development process*,[5] inspired by the boom of the information technology industry in the 1990s. The trend in computerization and internet base offers a powerful mode for dissemination of environmental information as well.[6]

To promote networking of environmental information, the Ministry of Environment and Forests established a program called Environmental Information System (ENVIS) in December 1982, to provide environmental information to Indian decision-makers, scientists, researchers, etc. The ENVIS nodes across the country have established a network to cover broad subject areas including environmental sciences, technology, and policy, including laboratories, government, non-government and educational institutions. The quality of environmental data collected by the pollution control boards, however, have several gaps (e.g. pollution effluents discharged by firm or industry are not available).

Formal environmental monitoring and enforcement of environmental regulations have also been weak in India. Thus civil society in India has played a significant role in the country's pollution control management. As noted in Chapter 7, community initiative is often through non-governmental organizations (NGOs) which have filed environmental writ petitions in the Indian courts and succeeded in establishing the polluter pays principle through some of the Supreme Court rulings. In settling these environmental cases, the Supreme Court, has, over the years, initiated reports to acquire information on sources of pollution, actual measure of the pollutants, compliance with existing regulations and the damage from pollution. Some of these reports have helped in formularizing subsequent government action. For instance, the 1999 Supreme Court High Powered Committee Report on Management of Hazardous Waste induced the pollution control boards to gather information on quantity of hazardous wastes processed/imported in India. (1995 Writ Petition No.657: filed by the NGO *Research Foundation for Science, Technology and Natural Resource Policy, New Delhi v. Union of India and others*).[7] In the event, the NGOs helped in the compilation and dissemination of environmental information, and the bolstering of environmental awareness in the economy.

Today, the Central Pollution Control Board has an NGO Cell to coordinate pollution control activities across the country. Besides establishing a network with State Pollution Control Boards/Zonal Offices, NGOs are provided with pollution testing kits and are offered financial assistance to organize mass awareness programs on environmental issues (CPCB Annual Report 2000-01: 102). The Ministry of Environment and Forests also supports NGOs engaged in promoting environmental education in the country, such as the Center for Environmental Education in Ahmedabad. Section 9.4 highlights some of the NGO activities in India, in the last decade, that have helped in the dissemination of environmental awareness or education.

9.3 Traditional Environmental Values and the Earth Charter

Environmental values have been ingrained in the lifestyle of Indians through community practices, food habits and even religious rites. While Chapter 5 briefly referred to the consumption pattern of people and how community food habits were ecologically sensitive, Chapter 8 touched on village community practices to preserve nature as something sacred. While the formal watershed in the institutionalization of environmental management took place in the 1970s, the protection and conservation of the environment have been mainstreamed into the lives of certain communities over several centuries! With nature being associated with day-to-day life, customs and religious practices, environmental conservation was built into the very fabric of Indian life. The preservation of some rich and biologically diverse regions (as in the Western Ghats) of the country has been attributed to these traditional practices.

In particular, sacred groves today are acknowledged as regions rich with native vegetation scattered across several villages in India. The species conserved in the sacred groves have been found to be those that perform key functions in the local ecosystem, and thus each sacred grove is unique in terms of the biological diversity it supports. Several NGOs in India have begun to create awareness of these sacred groves, and there have also been government initiatives to record the number of sacred groves in the country. Table 9.1 gives the list of sacred groves reported in different states of India.

Table 9.1 Reported Sacred Groves in India, 2001

State	Number of Sacred Groves
Andhra Pradesh	750
Arunachal Pradesh	58
Assam	40
Chattisgarh	600
Gujarat	29
Haryana	248
Himachal Pradesh	5000
Jharkhand	21
Karnataka	1424
Kerala	2000
Maharashtra	1600
Manipur	365
Meghalaya	79
Orissa	322
Rajasthan	9
Sikkim	56
Tamil Nadu	448
Uttaranchal	1
West Bengal	670
Total	*13720*

Source: CEE (2002) Chapter 10, Sacred Spaces: Traditions that Care for the Environment.

There are even attempts to mimic sacred groves in a scientific manner: the National Museum of Humankind, Bhopal, has a project to set up plots to replicate sacred groves, and help increase the awareness of the ecological and socio-economic significance of these groves to humankind (CEE 2002).

The execution of environmental protectionism with religious zeal in certain Indian communities is worth recording, as it reflects the ethos of the indigenous people, and also the scope of redefining that sentiment for environmental conservation today. The most noteworthy community with religious environmental fervor is that of the Bishnois. The Bishnoism faith has been practiced in India since the fifteenth century, and while it began in the deserts of Rajasthan, today its practice is also found in the states of Haryana, Gujarat, Madhya Pradesh and Uttar Pradesh. Bishnoism uses religion, a powerful medium, to help people imbibe the principle of conservation of nature in daily life (see Box 9.1).

Box 9.1 Religious Environmental Zeal of the Bishnois

The religious movement of Bishnoism is devoted to eco-friendliness and wildlife protection, and bond between man and nature. The religion provides a reference guide for the people to live in complete harmony with their environment. The Guru of this movement, Jambhoji, in the fifteenth century laid down 29 commandments to be practiced by the followers. Indeed the name Bishnoi is a literal conjugation of the number of principles {20 (Bis in Hindi) + 9 (No in Hindi)}. The principles include compassion for all living beings, cleanliness, devotion, vegetarian diet and truthfulness.

- Green trees are never to be cut, and can be used as timber only after trees age and die.
- Simple burial of the dead, so that the earth assimilates the flesh and wood for casket or cremation is saved.
- Wildlife is to be protected since they play a role in maintaining soil fertility and in holding the balance of harmful and beneficial life forms.
- Conserve water for use by man and animals by building tanks everywhere.
- Practice vegetarianism and be addicted to nothing – alcohol, tobacco or even tea.
- Do not seek alms or subsidy, from king or government. Believe in self-help.
- If ever you must choose to be violent, may it be in defense of a tree, an animal or your convictions; for this, even embrace death with cheer.

An incident in the Bishnoi history continues to be upheld and practiced even today. The story goes that in 1730, the Maharaja of Jodhpur, Abhay Singh (a local king) sent his men to the village of Khejadli to get timber as fuel for the lime kiln for the construction of his new palace. As the king's men began cutting the green trees, Amrita Devi and her three daughters resisted and were the first martyrs of the army. Following this, hundreds of women, men and children embraced the trees in defiance of the king's orders. It is believed that 360 Bishnois sacrificed their lives, and as the massacre continued they chanted one of their commandments: "Sar Santey Rookh Rahe To Bhi Sasto Jaan" (If a tree is saved even at the cost of one's head, it's worth it). On learning of this incident, the Maharaja apologized for the mistake committed by his officials and issued a royal decree prohibiting the cutting of trees and killing of wildlife in Bishnoi villages. The present Bishnoi communities in India have been active in preventing poachers from killing wildlife, even at the cost of their lives.

Sources: Bishnoi websites: http://www.bishnoi.org ; http://www.bishnoi.net.

While the tenets of the Bishnoi faith may seem rather severe or extreme, especially considering the zeal with which the practitioners have upheld them, the religion has had a remarkable impact on the environmental conservation movement within the country. Indeed, the pioneer of the twentieth-century Tree Hugging (*Chipko* in Hindi, literally hugging of trees to protect them from loggers) in the state of Uttar Pradesh, acknowledged that Bishnoism had served as the inspiration for this movement. The traditions of such communities continue to provide a lesson to modern-day environmentalists, on how a community strived to live in complete harmony with nature by incorporating environmental values in day-to-day living. For instance, the Earth Charter, an agreement among non-government participants from 78 countries, bears a remarkable resemblance to the compassionate principles of Bishnoism.

The global community of grassroots environmentalists established the Earth Charter in 2000, to encourage the incorporation of ecological sustainability in human life for a just and sustainable world. The principles in the Earth Charter resonate the values of traditional communities the world over, since practices from such communities across the globe were studied and drafted. Thus, it calls for values to promote interdependence of man and nature, ecological integrity, and compassionate living.[8] The Earth Charter represents the social movement to promote sustainable development, complementing the global economic fora on sustainability during the 1990s.

9.4 Role of NGOs in Environmental Information Dissemination

Over time economic and social change in India has been accompanied by an erosion of traditional community practices that were meant to conserve the natural environment; however now there is a parallel attempt to record and formalize the invaluable traditional knowledge and practices. Much of this effort has been with the help of non-governmental organizations (NGOs), which are playing a critical role in the collection and dissemination of environmental information in the country. This section briefly discusses the contribution of the environmental NGOs to the environmental management system in India, through the various roles played by them.

The number of environmental NGOs has increased rapidly in the last two decades, and at present there are almost 1,500 environmental NGOs in India. Most of these are located in the bigger states of Andhra Pradesh, Tamil Nadu, Uttar Pradesh, Maharashtra, Bihar, Orissa, and West Bengal. While many NGOs operate through urban offices, their agenda includes rural environmental management issues. They have been encouraging sound environmental management practices in both the industrial sector as well as in natural resources. The NGOs have also helped in voicing social environmental concerns in policy fora. No matter what the NGOs' role, the facilitation of environmental information has been a crucial aspect in each – whether as watchdogs of government policy, or industrial activity, or in directly educating entrepreneurs and consumers.

(i) Influencing Government Policies

Non-governmental organizations have helped bring about the enactment or amendment of environmental policies in India. While Chapter 7 highlighted the government policies following public interest litigations in the transport and industrial pollution sectors, there have been other instances where NGOs have facilitated policy changes through campaigns. One such success story where NGO action helped bring in remarkable policy change is in the area of medical waste management and handling.

An Indian NGO, Srishti, made an evaluation of municipal waste practices in 1995, and raised concerns about toxic chemical exposures, occupational health problems, inappropriate technologies, and unsanitary procedures in dealing with biomedical wastes. Support was solicited from citizen groups, healthcare professionals, and the government, followed by a national awareness tour on "dioxins". The NGO provided scientific information for a Supreme Court case, which in 1996 ordered the Central Pollution Control Board to devise technology standards for waste management. The NGOs began to work with manufacturers in 1997 to develop appropriate technologies and products for a small 30-bed hospital in Delhi, which Srishti used as a model. It was an effort to demonstrate the potential market size for products in environmental management like microwave machinery, autoclaves, waste shredders, colored non-PVC bags, bins, needle cutters, and worker safety gear. In 1998, the national law on Bio-Medical Rules made it mandatory for all institutional healthcare providers to segregate their waste in specified categories, disinfect the waste, transform discarded products so they could not be re-used, and safely dispose of all biomedical waste.

(ii) Monitoring Firm Behavior

Informal monitoring and enforcement of environmental regulations by the NGOs is considered to be an important feature of the pollution management regime in India. With the Supreme Court enforcing the polluter pays principle (in the environmental PILs) and ordering polluters to pay damages, polluting agents have been given the signal that inadequate formal monitoring notwithstanding, vigilance by the NGOs is a significant threat to reckon with. Even in the absence of legislative courses of action, the adverse publicity (for bad practice or violation of environmental norms) by such community groups can induce change in firm behavior, since bigger businesses do care about their public image!

In March 2001, Greenpeace found illegal dumping of toxic wastes at a mercury thermometer factory belonging to Hindustan Lever Limited (an Indian subsidiary of the Anglo-Dutch multinational, Unilever), at Kodaikanal. The factory, which was set up in 1983, had dumped the toxic mercury wastes outside the factory premises in sacks that subsequently spilled onto cultivated land, and put barefoot workers at risk.[9] The multinational corporation was accused of "double standards and shameful negligence by allowing its Indian subsidiary to dump several tons of highly toxic mercury waste" in the tourist resort of Kodaikanal and the surrounding protected nature reserve of Pambar Shola. In June 2001, three months after the exposure, the factory at Kodaikanal suspended its operations.

(iii) Imparting Environmental Education to Small Businesses

Besides monitoring government policies and business behavior, NGOs have helped to educate small enterprises on environmental issues. Small-scale industrial units (SSIs) in India contribute to a substantial portion of total industrial output and provide means of employment (albeit informal) to a large section of the urban poor. The three million SSIs employ nearly 16.7 million people, contribute to about 40% of total manufactured output, and account for 35% of India's total exports (CPCB Annual Report 2000-01: 216). At the same time, SSIs contribute substantially to total industrial effluents, particularly in the production of paper, sugar, leather and chemicals. The wastewater generated by SSIs is estimated to be about 40% of total effluents (ibid: 217). Thus pollution control in this sector can significantly reduce the total pollution load in the economy.

A Delhi-based NGO, the Society for Development Alternatives, has been working to help owners of small electroplating shop businesses to reduce waste and improve the working environment for employee health. Similarly, the Center for Resource Education, based in Hyderabad, works with a variety of small businesses and encourages them to reduce pollution in sectors including food processing, timber, steel, chemicals, and pharmaceuticals.

(iv) Market Signal with the Green Rating System

In order to help increase the knowledge of environmental characteristics of production systems and market products, a Green Ratings Project was initiated in the mid-1990s in India. The project was launched in 1996 by the Delhi-based Center for Science and Environment (CSE), with support from the MOEF and the UNDP. The first-of-its kind report was done for the Indian paper and pulp industry, and then more recently for the automobile industry.[10]

According to CSE, the recommendations of the first green ratings project helped in environmental upgradation. Many paper and pulp companies started buying wood from farm forestry rather than natural forest (sourcing from farm forestry increased from 60% in early 1999 to 80% in 2000). Similarly, water consumption per ton of paper produced declined by 16%, and ISO 14001 certification and process initiation increased during 1999-2000 among the paper plants.

As mentioned earlier, the green rating of the Indian automobile sector found that multinational companies do not fare better than Indian companies and current engine design is at least a decade old compared to similar types of vehicles in western countries. The latter finding corroborates with the time lag in the regulatory standard, viz. the Bharat II norms compare with Euro II standards that were implemented exactly a decade ago. This should prompt the Indian Government to check the regulatory gap in vehicle environmental standards.

(v) Aiding in Participatory Management of CPRs

The involvement of NGOs in the management of CPRs with local village communities has been more effective than government partnerships in both the forestry and watershed sectors (as discussed in Chapter 8). Village programs that are implemented by government officials have a more bureaucratic approach, and lose out with the villagers since government personnel have little or no training in social organization skills. An evaluation of watershed management projects covering 86 villages (in the states of Maharashtra and Andhra Pradesh) found that projects with NGO-component perform better, since they are more successful in promoting collective action (Kerr et al 2000). NGOs devote substantial time to social organization: in Andhra Pradesh some NGOs worked for years to help specific interest groups in a village organize themselves, creating a capacity for self-determination among even the poorest and politically weakest groups – something important for both sustainability and social equity of a new program. This kind of approach definitely helped to enforce agreements and implement the new institutional regime in those villages.

(vi) Protecting Indigenous Resources and Knowledge

Rural environmental management in India today has the active support of NGOs, not just for participatory management but also in the documentation and registration of traditional knowledge and innovations. Registration of such knowledge can help prevent bio-piracy like those experienced in the patents on wound-healing properties of turmeric, hypoglycemic properties of bitter gourd, and the fungicide property of neem. One such initiative is the People's Biodiversity Registers program with two institutions, Center for Ecological Sciences (of the Indian Institute of Science, Bangalore) and the Foundation for Revitalisation of Local Health Traditions. This was initiated in 1996, and in 1997, the first People's Biodiversity Register was released.

By 1998, 75 Plant Biodiversity Registers had been established with the help of the Indian Institute of Science and others. Other biodiversity registration initiatives in India include the Jaiv Panchayat, in 1999, by the Research Foundation of Science, Technology and Ecology, to establish definitive sovereignty of the local communities over their biodiversity resources. The Jaiv Panchayats are constituted of village volunteers, who inquire and record information on biological resources, and various uses of these resources in Community Biodiversity Registers. The first Jaiv Panchayat register was completed in Agasthyamuni village of Garhwal district in Uttar Pradesh, in June 1999 (WTO 2000a).

An Ahmedabad-based NGO, Society for Research and Initiatives for Sustainable Technologies and Institutions (*SRISTI*) established in 1993, has been documenting innovations developed by individuals at the village level. SRISTI has developed two databases: the *Institutional Innovations* database on indigenous ecological institutions for managing common property resources covering 22 countries; and the *Honey Bee* database of farmers' innovations and creative practices ("ecopreneurs"). This network documents the experiments and innovative uses of biological resources, and has probably the world's largest database on grassroots innovations (about 10,000) with names and addresses of the innovators, individuals or communities.[11] The collection of grassroots innovations is meant to develop, disseminate and reward practitioners of ecological resources.

Yet another NGO, Kalpavriksh, initiated documentation of various bio-resources used by community and conservation practices in the village of Jardhar of Teri Garhwal, in Uttar Pradesh, in 1995. A network of local farmers involved in reviving and spreading indigenous crop diversity (of Beej Bachao Aandolan – save the seeds campaign) collaborated with Kalpavriksh, whereby a copy of the register would be kept by both the villagers and by the NGO, and could be used and distributed only with consent of the villagers (WTO 2000b).

(vii) Enhancing Public Awareness

Enhancing public awareness in environmental issues is the first step to changing people's perspective and influencing their subsequent action. Thus some NGOs in India, like the Toxics Link (founded in 1996), collects and disseminates scientific information about the impact of toxins on people and the environment in local languages and formats that are accessible to a wide range of individuals, as well as grassroots and community groups. The organization consists of several decentralized regional nodes in the cities of Delhi, Mumbai, Bhavnagar and Chennai, with each node servicing information needs in their outreach areas.

The information network of such NGOs has been greatly facilitated by the internet in India. For instance, Toxics Link feeds information on international clean development and toxins in its local electronic networks, that serves as a clearing house on toxic information on an existing NGO electronic network, *India Link*.

In summing up the section, it should be noted that the state of environmental management in India would have been quite different, had it not been for the significant role played by NGOs. Environmental NGOs have influenced different aspects of environmental management in India. Be it a new bill on biological diversity, illegal dumping of wastes by factories, or educating small entrepreneurs, NGO activities have influenced government policy, industry activity and consumer preferences.

In a period of rapid and radical changes in India, the environmental aspects brought forth by the NGOs have led to the highlighting of social cost (and benefit) issues that the formal regulatory system and the market had failed to internalize. Essentially this has facilitated the revelation of environmental information of various economic activities or policies. Thus, from the perspective of the environmental economist, the NGOs play a vital role in the process of sustainable development, by increasing the environmental information set in the economic system.

Notes

[1] As mentioned in the earlier chapter, market distortions often result from government interventions meant to promote growth but which inadvertently induce more environmental pollution. For instance, the Indian Government's subsidizing of diesel (over petrol) to encourage freight, eventually promotes more carcinogenic diesel fumes as private vehicles also use diesel engines. Subsidized agricultural inputs like chemical fertilizers meant to enhance agricultural productivity eventually contaminate groundwater due to chemical run-off from the fields due to overuse.

[2] There are instances of private initiatives in the media too: a private television news channel began one-of-a-kind weather reporting, where the levels of air pollutants like suspended particulate matter, sulfur and nitrogen oxides were reported for major cities in India!

[3] India's agro-diversity is impressive: plant wealth is estimated to contain about 47,000 species constituting about 12% of the world's recorded flora (MOEF 2001: 81). Out of

these plant species, 5,150 are endemic with 2,532 species in the Himalayan region and 1,782 in peninsular India (ibid).

[4] Article 8(j) of the Convention on Biological Diversity encourages the parties to preserve and maintain knowledge, innovations and practices of indigenous and local communities embodying traditional lifestyles relevant for the conservation and sustainable use of biological diversity and promote their wider application with the approval and involvement of the holders of such knowledge, innovations and practices and encourage the equitable sharing of the benefits arising from the utilization of such knowledge, innovation and practices, Moreover, Article 10(c) indicates that parties should protect and encourage customary use of biological resources in accordance with traditional cultural practices that are compatible with conservation or sustainable use requirements.

[5] The growth of information technology in India can help integrate the remote villages, by providing access to information on prices of agricultural products, weather conditions, etc. This can aid the easier flow of knowledge, services and money across villages, and promote development. Indeed, the internet has begun to reach rural India in a small but significant manner. For example, Tarahaat is India's first such portal for farmers. Another case of IT application helping villagers to get the best market prices for agricultural output is found in the Dhar district of Madhya Pradesh, where 26 major centers are connected through an intranet network. The benefits reach over half a million people in more than 600 villages (CSE 2001a). The challenges for large-scale rural connectivity come from basic socio-economic factors like low level of literacy, lack of electricity and telecom infrastructure.

[6] According to a survey done by the National Association of Software and Service Companies (Nasscom), India's internet subscribers increased from 0.7 million subscribers in November 1998 to over 1.8 million subscribers by December 2000. More than 200 cities and towns in India have internet connectivity, as of December 2000, and there are five million personal computers. Thus, a base is being built in India to facilitate information flow across the country.

[7] Similarly, the 1999 Asim Barman Committee Report on "Solid Waste Management in Class 1 Cities in India" recommending a national waste management policy was used by the Supreme Court in issuing orders to national government and local bodies for keeping the cities clean. Subsequently this resulted in the *Municipal Solid Waste Management Rules* (2000). 1996 *Almitra H. Patel v. Union of India*, WP 888/1996 (2000.02.15) *Municipal Waste Case.*

[8] The Earth Charter was based on position papers and declarations of over 200 NGOs the world over, during the 1990s. The non-government agency, Development Alternatives, Delhi, was an active participant and contributor to the drafting of the Earth Charter. An Indian school, Delhi Public School, has utilized the Earth Charter to raise awareness among its students of sustainability principles.

[9] In a report presented to the Tamil Nadu Pollution Control Board, Unilever assessed the amount of mercury put out in the environment from its factory site at Kodaikanal at 539 kg (with a statistical variance "of between 43 kg minimum and 1,075 kg maximum"). Another 284 kg of mercury had been dispersed through "off site disposal". *HLL Factory at Kodaikanal Suspends Operations,* in website http://www.toxicslink.org.

[10] Among the attributes considered for the rating are engine design, pollution control equipment fitted, and emission test data. The most environmentally friendly vehicle in the car segment was found to be Daewoo's Matiz, followed by Maruti 800 (Euro II), followed by Hyundai's Santro. Honda City 1.5 V-tech was rated as the most technologically advanced and least-polluting vehicle in India.

[11] Website http://csf.colorado.edu/sristi.

Chapter 10

Conclusion

The economic planning exercise in India began in 1951 and true to the popular growth literature existing at the time, ignored the environmental dimension of the development process. Although the planners were aware of a choice between a heavy-industry-based versus a more village-oriented growth path, the former was chosen to achieve rapid economic growth.[1] It was only after two decades of industrialization that environmental regulation began to be enacted in a systematic manner for the first time in the country. Not surprisingly, the economic growth of the first few decades after independence left behind a legacy of environmental damage. It took an environmental disaster in the form of a toxic leakage from an industrial unit, to finally push the administration to establish a fully-fledged department in 1985. Since the mid-1980s domestic environmental legislation has been continuously enhanced.

Yet environmentalism had been an integral part of the traditional Indian way of life, as is evident from the age-old practices and customs of the indigenous population. In other words, an informal code of community norms had internalized environmental values in economic and social activities. The old order of life has been changing and India has been moving towards a more formal socio-economic system. This new order of life requires a more formal code of environmental values, which functions through regulations and markets. This is exactly the process that India is still evolving today. While the decade of the 1970s and 1980s saw the beginning of the process, the post-liberalization decade of the 1990s has accentuated the pace of the change.

The post-liberalization period has witnessed some of the most rapid and radical changes in the manner in which the environment is being integrated into the development path of India, some directly linked to global events and some intrinsically domestic. The analysis in the first six chapters has examined the impact of liberalization and globalization on environmental management in India in three tracks, namely: the regulatory, industrial and consumption sectors.

To begin with, environmental regulations have been strengthened following India's commitments in several multilateral environmental agreements and for export interest to match higher environmental standards in the major markets especially those in Western Europe and the US. In terms of industrial investment, liberalization has increased the flow of foreign capital for investment in a variety of industries. Although environmental and pollution standards in developed countries are more extensive and stringent than those in India, this fact does not seem to have been the guiding factor for attracting foreign investment. Indeed the investment and production trends in the polluting industries seem to be basically driven by large domestic market demand. In particular, the composition of FDI in India fails to support the pollution haven hypothesis since it shows no investment-bias in pollution-intensive industries. If anything, the "cleaner" information technology sector has been consistently attracting foreign capital in the past few years. More recently, the environment equipment and services sector in India has gained in significance (partly reflecting the enhancement of domestic environmental regulations) and the expected double-digit annual growth of the domestic environment market has made the sector attractive to foreign investors.

In terms of product and service specialization, the Indian export basket continues to have traditional exports (gems and jewelry, textiles, garments, food, engineering goods) and non-traditional software services as the important components, all of which are relatively "clean" sectors. At the same time, however, exports from polluting industries, like chemicals, have been consistently increasing, suggesting an emergence of specialization in specific polluting products. Yet this is not a feature unique to the globalization era, as the trend has been continuing since the 1970s.

At the firm level, liberalization has induced upgradation of production management systems and an increase in environmental certification; especially since importers in OECD countries (constituting the main destination countries of Indian exports) demand these as an assurance of good management practices and for compliance with their norms. The domestic environmental regulations and notification have also encouraged the use of environmental management tools (say, environmental impact assessment); however, the current implementation of such EIA practices has a long way to go. Industrial ecology, resource efficiency and minimization of waste generation, in a true sense, are yet to become an integral principle of the Indian industrial sector.

In the consumption sector, liberalization has been accompanied by a change towards a more pollution-intensive consumption basket. For example, liberalization has encouraged the use of private vehicles (the major source of urban air pollution) with an increasing number of models being offered in a country with a poor public transportation system. In this case, the cause of the increasing negative consumption externality stems from the existence of poor public transport systems in the country, and not trade per se. The one redeeming feature of this otherwise disturbing trend (of increasing emission per capita) is that the new range of vehicles in the post-globalization era is more energy efficient and therefore cleaner – i.e. on one hand, economic and demographic growth can be expected to add to the total pollution load, and on the other the pollution intensity of consumption (to some extent) can be expected to reduce as more environmentally friendly products enter into the domestic market. At the same time, however, consumption patterns in the Indian cities does reflect an increasing trend in pollution intensity of another kind. In terms of solid wastes, the composition of the urban solid waste indicates a significant jump in the use of non-biodegradable plastics and other toxic wastes.

On the other hand, globalization and the increasing commercialization of traditional knowledge have prompted the documentation and formalization of the indigenous environmental knowledge of India. Globalization is certainly driving Indians to re-evaluate the wealth of their culture and traditional knowledge, for example in the areas of farming practices and medicinal properties of certain species of plants, fruits and herbs. The vigor with which such knowledge is now being documented in India has been a unique feature of the globalization era.

At the same time, intrinsically domestic factors like environmental public interest litigations and judicial activism have prompted the implementation of the "polluter pays principle" through some of the landmark judgements emerging from the environmental PILs. Industry too has acknowledged that such environmental PILs and judicial activism have a nuisance value at the very least, and this has prompted abatement measures among the larger firms in the country.

In natural resource management, there has been a distinct shift towards greater community participation, beginning in the 1980s. The government endorsed this and also encouraged greater involvement of NGOs in the rural development process. There is finally a realization that environmental management through social change in attitudes and practice holds more promise, especially where the traditional growth-environment nexus has failed to make a difference. Community participation is an alternate way to internalize true social cost and the benefits of economic activities in the rural economy.

Public and community actions have played a rather significant role in evolving India's new environmental management system. Moreover, the new focus on environmental education and awareness that began in the 1990s is set to create an environmentally conscious Indian society that may not wait till a critical level of income or well-being is achieved before demanding higher environmental quality (if one believes in an environmental Kuznets curve). The emergence of the information age in India provides a unique complementary feature to the new environmental management system emerging in the country, namely a medium for facilitating environmental education and information dissemination. Rural information networking in particular can help bring accessibility to market knowledge and services to villages, so that the rural sector can experience development without the kind of environmentally costly urbanization so far witnessed in India.

While the foregoing analysis in this study is largely optimistic about the changes taking place in environmental management being in the right direction, one might stop to question what is indeed "clean". The conventional wisdom has been to categorize traditional heavy industries like chemicals, iron and steel, and distilleries, as "dirty". A growth path where the service sector begins to play the lead and the labor force is employed in high return services is very attractive; yet even such an economy requires some basic infrastructure and industrial development. So does the current export-led growth of the information technology (IT) sector in India provide a panacea to growth and development without the ugly environmental costs of dirty industries?

Yet as economists have always believed, there is indeed no free lunch, and the IT sector too poses serious environmental threats to the ecosystem. The e-waste generated by the hi-tech computer industry is known to be hazardous, since junked personal computers and accessories like printers and toner cartridges contain lead and heavy metals like cadmium, mercury and arsenic. Unless the growth of the domestic IT sector internalizes the environmental costs, the kind of environmental pollution experienced in India with the growth of traditional dirty sectors will be repeated. There is also a risk of the migration of hazardous computer wastes to a developing country like India.[2] Such a trade is based on the cost advantages of the recycling industry in the importing country, which typically ignores the environmental effects and toxic wastes released into land and water (i.e. pollution haven theory once more)! Thus while the focus has been disproportionately on "traditional" dirty industry in India, it is time that the non-traditional industry comes under scrutiny.

Another question that remains is whether the move towards environmental certification and labeling, that is becoming increasingly common in the global market place, can indeed ensure sustainable production? While India needs to learn from the good environmental practices of other countries, the features unique to her ecosystem also need to be incorporated in a path of sustainable growth. Although the country has made some progress in this direction, resource efficiency and minimization of pollution to ensure environmental efficiency is yet to become a feature of the Indian environmental regime. The current period can at best be termed a period of evolution of a new environmental management regime in India that integrates features of both global environmental practices and her very own traditional environmental values. This process of evolution will hopefully generate a sustainable development path unique to the country.

Notes

[1] The latter growth pattern was close to the Gandhian principles, and had been put forward by J. C. Kumarappa in his writings during the 1930s and 1940s (Why the Village Movement, 1938 and The Gandhian Economy and Other Essays, 1949). Kumarappa, as a representative of the All India Village Industries Association to the National Planning Commission in 1937, had put forward his model for agrarian society development. While his views had been rather extreme, he seems to have been the only Indian economist of his generation who had questioned the resource intensive pattern of industrialization in post-independence India (Guha 1992).

[2] In the US, it is estimated that e-wastes are generated at a rate of about 7 million tonnes per year due to the high obsolescence of computers and accessories. Moreover, since stringent regulations in the US do not allow these hazardous wastes to be dumped in landfills, they are being exported to developing countries like India. For instance, according to Greenpeace India, wastes imported from the World Trade Center into the country pose a serious risk of contamination from asbestos, PCBs (polychlorinated biphenyls), plastics, lead, mercury, and other contaminants from computers and fittings, in the 70,000 tons of scrap steel imported.

Bibliography

Adams, J. (1997) "Globalization, Trade and Environment", *Globalization and Environment: Preliminary Perspectives*, OECD: 179-98.

Agrawal, Arun and Elinor Ostrom (2000) *Collective Action, Property Rights and Devolution of Forest and Protected Area Management*, Yale University.

Agrawal, Arun and Gautam N. Yadama (1997) "How do Local Institutions Mediate the Impact of Market and Population Pressures on Resource Use? Van Panchayats in the Kumaon Himalayas, India", *Development and Change* 28(3): 435-65.

Anderson, Kym and Richard Blackhurst (1992) *The Greening of World Trade Issues*, Harvester Wheatsheaf, London.

Athreye, S.S. and Kapur, S. (2001) "Private Foreign Investment in India: Pain or Panacea", *The World Economy*, 24(3): 399-424.

Automeet-Autostatistics, website: http;//www.automeet.com/pop-06.html.

Banerjee, S. and S. Chattopadhyay (2001) "Globalization and Pollution Trade: The Indian Experience", presented at the Indian Statistical Institute, Bangalore.

Barfield (2001) "Free Trade and Sovereignty", The Fifth Column, *Far Eastern Economic Review*, 2001 (8): 28.

Barrett, Scott (1990) "The Problem of Global Environment Protection", *Oxford Review of Economic Policy* 6, Number 1.

Basant, Rakesh (2000) "Corporate Response to Economic Reforms", *Economic and Political Weekly* 35 (10), March: 813-822.

Batra, S.P. (2000) "Income Distribution and Consumer Durable Goods Markets", National Council of Applied Economic Research, New Delhi.

Baumol, William and Wallace E. Oates (1988) *The Theory of Environmental Policy*, Second Edition, Cambridge University Press.

Beck, Tony and Cathy Nesmith (2001) "Building on Poor People's Capacities: The Case of Common Property Resources in India and West Africa", *World Development*, Volume 29 (1): 119-133.

Behera, Chitta (2000) "Indegenising the Turtle Excluder Device for Indian Waters", *Kachhapa* Number 2: 9-11.

Berg, David R. and Grant Ferrier (1998) *Meeting the Challenge: The US Environment Industry Faces the 21st Century*, Office of Technology Policy, US Department of Commerce.

Bhagwati, Jagdish (1993) "Trade and the Environment: The False Conflict?" in Durwood Zaelke ed. *Trade and the Environment: Law, Economics and Policy*, Island Press, Washington.

Bhagwati, J and T.N. Srinivasan (1997) "Trade and the Environment: Does Environmental Diversity Detract from the Case for Free Trade?" in Bhagwati and Hudec ed. *Fair Trade and Harmonization: Prerequisites for Free Trade*, Volume 1, MIT Press.

Bhushan, R (2002) "Bold and Bisleri", *Business Line*, April 25.

Birdsall, Nancy and David Wheeler (1992) "Trade Policy and Industrial Pollution in Latin America: Where are the Pollution Havens?" in Patrick Low ed. *International Trade and the Environment*, World Bank Discussion Paper Number 159, pages 159-67.

Bowers, John (1997) *Sustainability and Environmental Economics: An Alternative Text*, Addison Wesley Longman Publishers.

Brander, J. and S. Taylor (1997) "International Trade Between Consumer and Conservationist Countries", *Resource and Energy Economics*, Volume 19: 321-44.

Brandon, C., K. Hommann and N.M. Kishor (1995) *The Cost of Inaction: Valuing the Economy-wide Cost of Environmental Degradation in India*, World Bank.

Bromley, Daniel W. (1989) "Property Relations and Economic Development: The Other Land Reform", *World Development* 17 (6): 867-77.

Business Line, Financial Daily from the Hindu group of publications.

CEE (2002) *Towards Sustainability: Learning from the Past, Innovations for the Future*, prepared for the Ministry of Environment and Forests, Center for Environment Education, Ahmedabad.

Census of India 2001, Government of India.

Chakravarty, Sukhamoy (1987) *Development Planning*, Oxford University Press.

Charnovitz, Steve (2002) *International Standards and the WTO*, background paper for the Global Forum on Trade, Environment and Development, Quito, June.

Chichilnisky, G. (1994) "North-South Trade and the Global Environment", *American Economic Review*, September: 851-74.

Chopra, K. (2000) "Environmental Issues in South Asia: Theory, Policy and Institutions for Governance", Institute of Economic Growth, Working Paper, July.

Chopra, K. and S.C. Gulati (1998) "Environmental Degradation, Property Rights and Population Movements: Hypothesis and the Evidence from Rajasthan", *Environment and Development Economics* 3: 35-57.

Chudnovsky, Daniel and Andres Lopez (1999) *TNCs and the Diffusion of Environmentally Friendly Technologies to Developing Countries*, UNCTAD.

CII (1996) *Environmental Business Opportunities in India*, Confederation of Indian Industry, New Delhi.

CII (1999) *Directory of Environmental Enterprises in India,* Confederation of Indian Industry, New Delhi.

CMIE (various years) *Monthly Review of the Indian Economy* (October, November), Economic Intelligence Service, Center for Monitoring Indian Economy.

Coase, Ronald (1960) "The Problem of Social Cost", *Journal of Law and Economics 3*, reprinted in Dorfman and Dorfman ed. (1993) *Economics of the Environment*, W.W. Norton and Company: 109-138.

Cole, Mathew A. and Eric Neumayer (2002) *Economic Growth and Environment in Developing Countries: What are the Implications of the Environmental Kuznets Curve?*, London School of Economics.

Compendium of Environmental Statistics 2000, Central Statistical Organization, India, 2001. (http://www.nic.in/stat/compenv2000.htm).

Copeland, B. and S. Taylor (1994) "North-South Trade and the Environment", *Quarterly Journal of Economics*, August, 755-87.

CPCB (1999a) *Status of Water Supply, and Wastewater Generation, Collection, Treatment and Disposal in Class I Cities*, CUPS/44/1999-2000, Central Pollution Control Board, New Delhi.

CPCB (1999b) *Status of Solid Waste Generation, Collection, Treatment and Disposal in Metrocities*, CUPS/46/1999-2000, Central Pollution Control Board, New Delhi.

CPCB (1999c) *Status of Municipal Solid Waste Generation, Collection, Treatment and Disposal in Class I Cities*, CUPS/48/1999-2000.

CPCB (1999d) *Status of Water Supply, and Wastewater Generation, Collection, Treatment and Disposal in Class II Cities*, CUPS/49/1999-2000, Central Pollution Control Board New Delhi.

CPCB (2000) *Air Quality Status and Trends in India*, NAAQMS/14/1999-2000, Central Pollution Control Board and Ministry of Environment and Forests, New Delhi.

CPCB (2000a) *White Paper on Pollution in Delhi with an Action Plan*, Central Pollution Control Board (website: http://envfor.nic.in/divisions/cpoll/delpolln.html).

CPCB (2001) *Annual Report 2000-01*, Central Pollution Control Board and Ministry of Environment and Forests, New Delhi.

Cropper, Maureen L. and Wallace E. Oates (1992) "Environmental Economics: A Survey", *Journal of Economic Literature*, Volume XXX, June: 675-740.

Cropper, M., N. Simon, A. Alberini, and K. Sharma (1999) "The Health Effects of Air Pollution in Delhi", Working Paper, World Bank, Washington D.C.

CSE (1998) "Turning Turtle" and "Trouble in the Deep", *Down to Earth*, Volume 7, Number 2, June 15.

CSE (1999) *The Citizen's Fifth Report on the State of the Environment*, Centre for Science and Environment, New Delhi.

CSE (2001a) "Rural Infotech: Virtually There", *Down to Earth*, Volume 9, Number 18, February 15, Centre for Science and Environment, New Delhi.

CSE (2001b) "India Organics Inc.", *Down to Earth*, September 15: 39-41.

Dasgupta, Partha (1997) *Environmental and Resources Economics in the World of the Poor*, Special Address at RFF 1997 board meeting.

Dasgupta, Partha and Karl-Goran Maler (1994) "Poverty, Institutions and the Environmental Resource-Base", reprinted in Berhman and Srinivasan ed. *Handbook of Development Economics*, Volume 3.

Dean, Judith (1992) "Trade and the Environment: A Survey of the Literature", in Patrick Low ed. *International Trade and the Environment*, World Bank Discussion Paper 159, The World Bank: 15-28.

DOC (2002) *Annual Report 2001-02*, Department of Commerce, Government of India.

Dorfman, Robert and Nancy S. Dorfman (1993) *Economics of the Environment: Selected Readings*, 3rd edition, W.W. Norton and Company.

Down to Earth (various issues), Center for Science and Environment, New Delhi.

Dreze, J. and M. Murthi (2000) "Fertility, Education and Development: Further Evidence from India", *The Development Economics Discussion Paper Series 20*, LSE.

Durning, Alan (1992) *How Much is Enough?*, Earthscan, London.

EC (2000) *Organic Farming: Guide to Community Rules*, European Community.

Economic Survey of India (various years), Ministry of Finance, Government of India.

Ehrlich, P., G. Wolff, G. Daily, J. Hughes, S. Daily, M. Dalton and L. Goulder (1999) "Knowledge and the Environment" *Ecological Economics* 30, 267-284.

Environmental, Business International, Inc. Website: http://www.ebiusa.com.

Esty, Daniel C. (1994) *Greening the GATT: Trade, Environment and the Future*, Institute for International Economics.

Esty, Daniel C. (1999) *Globalization and the Environment in Asia*, Yale University, and Marie Pangestu Center for Strategic International Studies.

Esty, Daniel C. and Michael E. Porter (1998) "Industrial Ecology and Competitiveness: Strategic Implications for the Firm", *Journal of Industrial Ecology*, Volume 2, Number 1: 35 – 43.

EXIM (2002) *Agro & Processed Foods: A Sector Study*, Export and Import Bank of India.

EXIMIUS (2001) "India's Organic Food Exports: Problems and Prospects", Vl XV, Issue III, September: 9-12 (www.eximbankindia.com/september-2001.pdf).

FAO (1997) "Towards Safe and Effective Use of Chemicals in Coastal Aquaculture", Joint Group of Experts on the Scientific Aspects of Marine Environmental Protection, *Report and Studies No. 65*, Food and Agricultural Organization, Rome.

Fedriksson, P. and M. Mani (2001) *Trade Integration and Political Turbulence: Environmental Policy Consequences*, Southern Methodist University and International Monetary Fund.

Ferrantino, M. (1997) "International Trade, Environmental Quality and Public Policy", *World Economy*, Volume 20: 43-72.

Ferrier, Grant (2000) *Environmental Industry Evolution Sets Up the Next Industrial Revolution: Resource Productivity is the Key to Future Market Development*, January. http://www.environews.com.

Fontagne, Lionel, Friedrich von Kirchbach and Mondher Mimouni (2001) *A First Assessment of Environmental Related Trade Barriers*, CEPII, Document No. 01-10, October.

Foster, Andrew D. and Mark R. Rosenzweig (2002) "Economic Growth and the Rise of Forests", *PIER Working Paper* 02-028.

Frontline, National magazine from The Hindu, http://www.frontlineonnet.com.

Gadgil, Madhav (1998) "Traditional Resource Management Systems" in Baidyanath Saraswati ed. *Lifestyle and Ecology*, IGNCA, New Delhi.

Gadgil, Madhav (2001) *Ecological Journeys: The Science and Politics of Conservation in India*, Permanent Black, India.

GATT Report (1992) *Trade and Environment*, GATT, Geneva, February.

Guha, Ramchandran (1992) "Prehistory of Indian Environmentalism: Intellectual Traditions", *Economic and Political Weekly*, January 4-11: 57-64.

Gupta, Anil (2000) "Rewarding Traditional Knowledge and Contemporary Grassroots Creativity", paper presented at the seminar *Traditional Knowledge and IPRs*, Harvard University.

Grossman, Gene. and Alan Krueger (1991) "Environmental Impacts of a North-American Free Trade Agreement", NBER Working Paper No. 3914.

Grossman, Gene and Alan Krueger (1994) *Economic Growth and the Environment*, NBER Working Paper No. 4634.

Hahn, Robert W. and Robert N. Stavins (1992) "Economic Incentives for Environmental Protection: Integrating Theory and Practice", *American Economic Review*, 82(2), May: 464-468.

Hardin, Garrett (1968) "The Tragedy of the Commons", *Science* 162: 1243-48, reprinted in Dorfman and Dorfman ed. *Economics of the Environment*, op. cit. 3rd edition: 5-19.

Hartman, Raymond S., Mainul Huq and David Wheeler (1997) "Why Paper Mills Clean Up: Determinants of Pollution Abatement in Four Asian Countries", *World Bank Policy Research Working Paper 1710*.

Heil, M. and T.M. Selden (2001) "International Trade, Intensity and Carbon Emissions: A Cross-Country Econometric Analysis", *Journal of Environment and Development* 10: 35-49.

Hettige, H., M. Huq, S. Pargal and D. Wheeler (1996) "Determinants of Pollution Abatement in Developing Countries", World Bank.

Hotelling (1931) "The Economics of Exhaustible Resources", *Journal of Political Economy*, reprinted in Adrian C. Darnell ed. *The Collected Economics Articles of Harold Hotelling*, Springer-Verlag, 1990: 64-90.

IGCC (2001) *Study on the Indian Environmental Scenario and Market*, Indo-German Chamber of Commerce, Bombay, February.

ISO (2002) *The ISO Survey of ISO 9000 and ISO 14000 Certificates: Eleventh Cycle*, International Organization for Standardization.

Jaffe, A., S. Peterson, P. Rodney and R. Stavins (1995) "Environmental Regulation and the Competitiveness of US Manufacturing: What does the Evidence Tell Us?", *Journal of Economic Literature*, Volume 33: 133-63.

James, A. J. (1996) "Using Environmental Policy Instruments: A Review of Theory and International Practice" in Murty *et al* ed. *Economic Instruments and Other Instruments for Water Pollution Abatement*, Institute of Economic Growth, New Delhi: 50-82.

Jayaram, Raji and Peter Lanjouw (1999) "The Evolution of Poverty and Inequality in Indian Villages", *The World Bank Research Observer* 14, January.

Jha, A. (1997) "Protection of the Environment, Trade and India's Leather Exports" in Veena Jha, Grant Hewison and Maree Underhill ed. *Trade, Environment and Sustainable Development: A South Asian Perspective*, Macmillan Press: 117-122.

Jodha, N.S. (1990) "Depletion of Common Property Resources in India: Micro-Level Evidence", *Population and Development Review* Volume 15 supplement.

Jodha, N.S. (1995) "Common Property Resources and the Environmental Context: Role of Biophysical versus Social Stresses", *Economic and Political Weekly*, December 23: 3278-2383.

Kachhapa (2000) "Activities in Orissa", *Kacchapa* Issue #3, October.

Kumarappa, J.C. (1938) *Why the Village Movement?*, All India Village Industries Association.

Kumarappa, J.C. (1949) *The Gandhian Economy and Other Essays*, Wardha Associations.

Kerr, J., G. Pangare, V. L. Pangare and P. J. George (2000) "An Evaluation of Dryland Watershed Development Projects in India", *EPTD Discussion Paper 68*, International Food Policy Research Institute, Washington.

Kolavalli, S. and John Kerr (2002) "Mainstreaming Participatory Watershed Development", *Economic and Political Weekly*, January 19: 225-242.

Kumar, P. and S.C. Aggarwal (2001) "Does Environmental Kuznets Curve Exist for Changing Land Use?: Empirical Evidence from Major States of India", paper presented in conference *Path to Sustainability: Theory and Practice*, US Society for Ecological Economics, Duluth, Minnesota, July.

Legal and Scientific Resources for Asia (website: www.elaw.org.resources).

Lele, Sharachchandra (2000) "Godsend, sleight of hand, or just muddling through: joint water and forest management in India", *Natural Resource Perspectives*, Number 53, Overseas Development Institute, London.

Low, Patrick (ed.) (1992) *International Trade and the Environment*, World Bank Discussion Papers 159, World Bank, Washington D.C.

Low, Patrick and Raed Safadi (1992) "Trade Policy and Pollution", in Low ed. *International Trade and the Environment*, World Bank Discussion Papers 159, World Bank: 29-52.

Lucas, Robert, David Wheeler and Hemamala Hettige (1992) "Economic Development, Environmental Regulation and the International Migration of Toxic Industrial Pollution: 1960-1988" in Patrick Low ed. *International Trade and the Environment*, World Bank Discussion Papers 159, World Bank.

Mani, M., S. Pargal and M. Huq (1997) *Is There an Environmental "Race to the Bottom"? Evidence on the Role of Environmental Regulation in Plant Location Decisions in India*, World Bank.

Mani, M. and D. Wheeler (1997) "In Search of Pollution Havens? Dirty Industry in the World Economy 1960-1995", Policy Research Department, World Bank, Washington D.C.

Markandya, Anil, Patrice Harou, Lorenzo G. Bellu and Vito Cistulli (2002) *Environmental Economics for Sustainable Growth: A Handbook for Practitioners*, The World Bank, Edward Elgar Publishing Ltd.

Meadows, D.H., D.L. Meadows, and J. Randers (1992) *Beyond the Limits: Confronting the Global Collapse, Envisioning a Sustainable Future*, Chelsea Green Publishing Co.

Meadows, D.H., D.L. Meadows J. Randers and W.J. Behrens (1972) *The Limits to Growth*, Universe Books, N.Y.

Menon, P. and R. Ramachandran (1997) "Contamination Scare: Indian Seafood Exports", *The Week Magazine*, August 24.

MFPI (2002) *Annual Report 2001-02*, Ministry of Food Processing Industries, India.

Ministry of Agriculture (2002) *Aquaculture Authority News*, Volume 1, Number 1, September.

MOEF (1993) *Environment Action Programme: India*, Ministry of Environment and Forests, New Delhi.

MOEF (2001) *India State of the Environment Report 2001*, Ministry of Environment and Forests, New Delhi.

MOEF (2002) *Annual Report 2000-01, 2001-02,* Ministry of Environment and Forests, New Delhi.

MOEF (2003) *Annual Report 2002-03,* Ministry of Environment and Forests, New Delhi.

Myers, Norman and Jennifer Kent (2000) "New Consumers: The Influence of Affluence on the Environment", report to the Winslow Foundation, Washington D.C.

Nagaraj, R. (2000) "Indian Economy since 1980: Virtuous Growth or Polarisation?", *Economic and Political Weekly*, August 5, 2831-38.

Nambiar, R.G., B.L. Mungekar, and G.A. Tadas (1999) "Is Import Liberalisation Hurting Domestic Industry and Employment?", *Economic and Political Weekly*, February 13.

Nasscom (2002) *Software Industry in India 2001-02*, National Association of Software and Service Companies, India.

Nasscom-McKinsey Report (2002) *Strategies to Achieve the Indian IT Industry's Aspirations*, June.

Nyati, K. P. (2000) "ISO 14001 in India – Boon or Blackmail", paper presented at the 2nd *Environment Summit*, CII, New Delhi.

Oates, Wallace (1994) "Environment and Taxation: The Case of The United States" in OECD document *Environment and Taxation: The Case of The Netherlands, Sweden and The United States.* Reprinted in Wallace, Oates (ed) *The Economics of Environmental Regulation*, Edward Elgar Publishing Ltd, 1996: 195-230.

O'Connor, David (1995) *Applying Economic Instruments in Developing Countries: From Theory to Implementation*, OECD Development Centre, Paris, France.

Panayotou, Theodore (1992) *Empirical Tests and Policy Analysis of Environmental Degradation at Different Stages of Economic Development*, Harvard Institute of International Development.

Panayotou, Theodore (2000) "Globalization and Environment", *CID Working Paper No. 53*, Center for International Development, Harvard University.

Pargal, S., M. Mani and M. Huq (1997) "Inspections and Emissions in India: Puzzling Survey Evidence", Policy Research Division, *Working Paper 1810*, World Bank.

Pargal, S. and D. Wheeler (1995) "Informal Regulation of Industrial Pollution in Developing Countries: Evidence from Indonesia", Policy Research Division, *Working Paper 1416*, World Bank.

Parivesh (2001) Newsletter of the Central Pollution Control Board of India, New Delhi.

Paulus, Stephan (1995) *Market Based Instruments in Environmental Policy in Developing Countries*, Framework for Policy Planning and Institutional Development in Environment, GATE, Germany.

Pearce, David (1995) *Blueprint 4: Capturing Global Environmental Value*, Earthscan Publications, London.

Pearce, David and Edward Barbier (2000) *Blueprint for A Sustainable Economy*, Earthscan Publications, London.

Pearce, David and Jeremy J. Warford (1993) *World Without End: Economics, Environment and Sustainable Development*, World Bank, Oxford University Press.

Pearson, Charles S. (2000) *Economics and the Global Environment*, Cambridge University Press.

Pethig, Rudiger (1976) "Pollution, Welfare, and Environmental Policy in the Theory of Comparative Advantage", in the *Journal of Environmental Economics and Management* 2: 160-69.

Pezzey, John (1989) "Economic Analysis of Sustainable Growth and Sustainable Development", *Working Paper 15*, Environment Department, World Bank, Washington D.C.

Pigou, Arthur (1932) *The Economics of Welfare*, 4th edition, Macmillan, London.

Prakash, B.K. (2001) "Benefits Accrued on Effective Implementation and Certified Performance Management Systems in Quality, Environment and Social Accountability", Exports & Corporate Management Division, *Prem Group of Companies*, Tirupur, India.

Pretty, Jules and Rachel Hine (2001) "Reducing Food Poverty with Sustainable Agriculture: A Summary of New Evidence", Final report from the Safe-World, University of Essex, UK.

Rao, K. S. C., M.R. Murthy and K. V. K. Ranganathan (1999) "FDI in the Post Liberalisation Period: An Overview", *Journal of Indian School of Political Economy*, Volume XI, Number 4, July-September.

RBI (2001) *Handbook of Statistics on Indian Economy 2001*, Reserve Bank of India.

RBI (various years) *Annual Report*, Reserve Bank of India.

Regens, James L. and Robert W. Rycroft (1988) *The Acid Rain Controversy*, University of Pittsburg Press.

Repetto, Robert (1994) *The Second India Revisited: Population, Poverty and Environmental Stress over Two Decades*, World Resources Institute, Washington D.C.

Robins, Nick (2000) *Making Sustainability Bite: Transforming Global Consumption Patterns*, International Institute for Environment and Development.

Rock, Michael T. (1996) "Pollution Intensity of GDP and Trade Policy: Can the World Bank be Wrong?", *World Development*, Volume 24, Number 3, 471-479.

Ruud, Audun (2002) "Environmental Management of Transnational Corporations in India – Are TNCs Creating Islands of Environmental Excellence in a Sea of Dirt?", *Business Strategy and the Environment*, Volume 11, Issue 2: 103-118.

Saigal, Sushil (2001) *Joint Forest Management: A Decade and Beyond*, JFM website: http://www.rupfor.org/ns-furthr-rdg/jfm-nationaloverview.doc.

Sathe, S.P. (2002) *Judicial Activism in India: Transgressing Borders and Enforcing Limits*, Oxford University Press.

Sawhney, Aparna (1997a) "A Review of Market-Based Instruments for Pollution Control: Implications for India", *NIPFP Working Paper Number 2*, and background paper for Ministry of Environment and Forests "Taskforce Report to Evaluate Market Based Instruments for Industrial Pollution Abatement".

Sawhney, Aparna (1997b) *Administration of Environmental Regulations and Tax Incentives*, chapter prepared for UNDP Report, NIPFP, New Delhi.

Sawhney, Aparna (1999) "Development and the Environment" in Phillip O'Hara ed *Encyclopedia of Political Economy*, Routledge, Volume 1: 196-99.

Sawhney, Aparna (2002) "Sanitary and Phytosanitary Measures in India", country paper presented in the APO *Seminar on Sanitary and Phytosanitary Measures*, Tokyo, December.

Sawhney, Aparna (2003a) "Public Interest Litigation as Indirect Market-Based Instrument of Pollution Control", *Economic and Political Weekly*, Volume 38, Number 1: 32-37.

Sawhney, Aparna (2003b) "How Environmental Provisions Affect Asian Developing Countries", *Management Review*, Volume 15, Number 1: 11-18.

Scitovsky, Tibor (1954) "Two Concepts on External Economies", *Journal of Political Economy* 62: 143-51.

Scitovsky, Tibor (1976) *The Joyless Economy*, Oxford University Press.

Scitovsky, Tibor (1986) *Human Desire and Economic Satisfaction*, Wheatsheaf Books.

Sethi, R. and E. Somanathan (1996) "The Evolution of Social Norms in Common Property Resource Use", *American Economic Review* 86(4): 766-88.

Shaman, David (1996) *India's Pollution Regulatory Structure and Background*, World Bank.

Smarzynska, Beata K. and Shang-Jin Wei (2001) "Pollution Havens and Foreign Direct Investment: Dirty Secret or Popular Myth?", *World Bank Working Paper 2673*, September.

SOL-Survey (2001) *Organic Agriculture World-Wide: Statistics and Future Prospects*, SOL-IFOAM, International Federation of Organic Agricultural Movements.

Solow, Robert (1993) "Sustainability: An Economist's Perspective" in Dorfman and Dorfman ed. *Economics of the Environment*: 179-87, op.cit.

Srishti-Toxics Link (200) "Trojan Horses: Persistent Organic Pollutants in India", a Srishti and Toxics Link Report, November.

Stern, David and Michael Common (2001) "Is there an Environmental Kuznets Curve for Sulfur?", *Journal of Environmental Economics and Management*, 41: 162-178.

Stern, David, Michael Common and Edward Barbier (1996) "Economic Growth and Environmental Degradation", *World Development* 24(7), 1151-60.

Stevens, Candice (1993) "The Environmental Effects of Trade", *The World Economy*, Volume 16, Number 4: 439-452.

Sundaram, K (2001) "The Employment – Unemployment Situation in India in the 1990s", *CDE Working Paper Number 88*, February, Delhi School of Economics.

Suri, V. and D. Chapman (1998) "Economic Growth, Trade and Energy: Implications for the Environmental Kuznets Curve", *Ecological Economics* 25: 195-208.

TERI Newsletter (various issues), The Energy Research Institute, New Delhi.

TERI Yearbook 2001, The Energy Research Institute, New Delhi.

UNDP (1999) *Human Development Report*.

UNDP (2002) *Human Development Report*, Oxford University Press.

UNEP (2002) Sustainable Consumption: A Global Status Report, United Nations Environment Programme, DTIE, Production and Consumption Branch.

USDOC (2001) "Leading Sectors for US Exports and Investment", Chapter 5 in *India: Country Commercial Guide FY 2002*, US Department of Commerce.

USDOC (2002) *US Country Commercial Guide for India 2003*, United States Department of Commerce.

USFDA (2001-2002) *Monthly Import Refusal Reports*, Operational and Administrative System for Import Support (OASIS), United States Food and Drug Administration.

Veen-Groot, D.B. van, and Peter Nijkamp (1999) "Globalisation, Transport and the Environment: New Perspectives for Ecological Economics", *Ecological Economics* 31, 331-346.

Wackernagel, Mathis, Chad Monfreda and Diana Deumling (2002) *Ecological Footprint of Nations November 2002 Update*, Redefining Progress, California.

Wackernagel, M., L. Onisto, A.C. Linares, I. López Falfán, J. Méndez Garcia, A. Suárez Guerrero, Ma. G. Suárez Guerrero (1997) *Ecological Footprints of Nations*, Earth Council. website: http://www.ecouncil.ac.cr/rio/focus/report/english/footprint.

Wheeler, David (2001) "Racing to the Bottom", *Journal of Environment and Development*, Volume 10 (3): 225-245.

World Bank (1992) *World Development Report: Development and the Environment*, World Bank, Washington D.C.

World Bank (2000) *Greening Industry: New Roles for Communities, Markets, and Governments*, A World Bank Policy Research Report, Oxford University Press.

World Development Indicators, various years, World Bank, Washington D.C.

WRI (2002) *World Resources*, World Resources Institute, Washington D.C.

WTO (1996) "The Effect of Environmental Measures on Market Access", *Non-paper by India*, CTE, June 20.

WTO (1998) *Environmental Benefits of Removing Trade Restrictions and Distortions*, Note by Secretariat (Addendum), WT/CTE/W/67/Add.1, March.

WTO (1999) *Trade and Environment*, Special Studies 4.

WTO (2000a): "Protection of Biodiversity and Traditional Knowledge – The Indian Experience", WT/CTE/W/156 IP/C/W/198, submitted by India, July 14, 2000.

WTO (2000b) "The Study of the Effects of Environmental Measures on Market Access", *WT/CTE/W/177*, Communication from India, October 27.

WTO (2001-1997) "Environmental Database", WT/CTE/W46, WT/CTE/W77, WT/CTE/W118, WT/CTE/W143, and WT/CTE/W195.

Xu, Xinpeng (1999) "Do Stringent Environmental Regulations Reduce the International Competitiveness of Environmentally Sensitive Goods? A Global Perspective", *World Development*, Volume 27, Number 7, 1215-1226.

Zarsky, Lyuba (1999) "Havens, Halo and Spaghetti: Untangling the Evidence about Foreign Direct Investment and the Environment", in *Foreign Direct Investment and the Environment*, OECD: 47-74.

Index

Notes: bold page numbers refer to tables; numbers in brackets preceded by *n* are note numbers.